Seismic Stages

For Barbara, May 2000 -
... one who knows the same roads as our
roads and keeps on going, and doing,
and making. Love - Elizabeth
& Carl

ALSO BY BISHOP & FULLER:

Mating Cries
Wordworkers, 1998

Marie Antoinette
Wordworkers, 1994

Loveplay
Wordworkers, 1993

Family Snapshots [audioplay]
The Independent Eye, 1994

Tapdancer [audioplay]
The Independent Eye, 1992

Rash Acts: 18 Snapshots for the Stage
Wordworkers, 1989

The Want Ads [audioplay]
The Independent Eye, 1988

Full Hookup
Dramatists Play Service, 1982

For complete listing and summaries of 50+ Bishop/Fuller plays available in typescript, visit The Independent Eye's webpage at www.independenteye.org.

Conrad Bishop & Elizabeth Fuller

Seismic Stages

Five Plays for Teens

an anthology of plays and sketches created by The Independent Eye

WordWorkers

Sebastopol, CA

Seismic Stages
Five Plays for Teens

All public performances are subject to royalty. This does not include in-class performances for teaching purposes, but it does include performances in school for a student body beyond class size. Except for in-class use, written permission is required for performance, including readings and excerpts. Contact:

The Independent Eye
1-800-357-6016
eye@independenteye.org

First Printing June 2000
ISBN: 0-9624511-7-7
Library of Congress Catalog Card Number: 99-91942

Contents

Thanks

To the Franklin Institute and Point Breeze Performing Arts Center, and to Roberta Cooks, Mark Hallen, Connie Norwood, Joyce Willis, Bert Nelson, Amy Gorbey, Catharine Slusar, and Donna Brown.

To the students of Dallastown High School, Dallastown, PA, and the staff of Self Help Counseling & Educational Center.

To Sam Reynolds, Joyce Willis, Kareem Carpenter, and Hugh Choi, and members of The Independent Eye's Genesis Ensemble.

To the students of Germantown Academy, Agnes Irwin School, and University of the Arts, and to Kevin Augustine, Tim Jackson, Chris Kendra, Joy Keys, Sonja Robson, and J.J. Van Name.

To the members of Milwaukee's Theatre X from 1969 to 1974 for creative contribution to early versions of three sketches included here.

To Carole Haas and members of our Board of Trustees for generous support of our school projects; and to the Pew Charitable Trusts, Pennsylvania Council on the Arts, and National Endowment for the Arts for supplemental project support.

Preface

In our view, the best "plays for teens" have been written by Shakespeare, Molière, Brecht, Ibsen, Chekhov, Euripides and hundreds of other playwrights over the past 2,500 years. Adolescence is a time of discovery, and there's no richer landscape of human behavior and spirit than the world's dramatic literature. The work of teenagers is not learning how to become teenagers, but how to be men and women.

So the plays and sketches included in this collection are far from being the "best" dramatic work for teenagers. We offer these plays for a more targeted purpose: to expand the repertoire of work that can be performed in regular high schools — not only those with superlative drama programs — by and for students. We also hope they can be seen as models of work that can be created *within* schools through collective methods.

All the work included here is a product of collective creation. The Independent Eye provided direction and final scripting, but each piece was strongly infused by the improvisations and impulses of many participating actors. Sometimes a group was led in free-form improvisations around a scenario, leading to a script. Sometimes a script evolved over a span of several years, with new cast members bringing fresh insights. Always, the audiences taught us what the show was about.

In that spirit, we welcome experiment with the texts of these pieces. The normal requirement in production agreements is to perform a play exactly as written, no line changes. Usually, we too insist on that. But for these plays, we invite you to bring your own creative energies to the text as well as to the performance.

You may change lines to update colloquialisms. You may add new character lines. You may even improvise new scenes. In those plays involving direct questions to the audience, you may find questions that are more provocative and relevant than those written here.

But you may make changes in the text only if you agree to three conditions:

1. Don't change a single word unless you really feel you understand why it was written that way in the first place.

2. Add elements only if they add truth to the piece, make the characters richer, or bring it closer to the understanding of your audience.

3. If you make changes, send us a copy of the script.

Why should we offer this freedom? After all, we've worked hard in crafting the plays, and they've been tested in performance. We'd hardly relish the discovery that our work has been mangled — with our own permission — into some embarrassing shadow of itself.

But if these plays are to work for you, they'll work only because they're fully alive, because you've made it *yours*. That doesn't mean you need to change lines; it *does* mean that you say a line because, collectively, you feel that that's the best way to say it. An unexamined play isn't worth performing.

Of course, if you want to alter the whole intent of the work, e.g. adding a speech with some explicit moral or political twist clearly counter to our aim, then you should write your own play.

But if there are questions in your mind about changes, or about interpretation in general, there's a proven magical technique. *Ask us.* We're accessible by phone or by email and welcome inquiries from anyone who's dedicated to doing the best possible job. For us, audiences are audiences, whether they're Off-Broadway or at Susquehannock High School.

One final word about interpretation. Because much of this work is comic, and because characters are often delineated with a few brush-strokes, it's easy for actors to fall into stereotype. Always assume, though, that the characters are as smart as you are, and as human. When characters reduce themselves to stereotype, it's because real people do that. If they persist in doing supremely stupid things, that may make them absurd or pathetic, but it doesn't make them less human. Find their incongruities, their contradictions and inconsistencies. That's the first step to loving them, which is the first step to playing them.

— Conrad Bishop & Elizabeth Fuller

A Friend from High School

Characters

Carrie. 19. Waitress.

Joy. 20. College student.

Gil. 23. Auto mechanic.

The Hacker. An energetic man in a sport jacket and tie.

The actress playing Carrie begins and ends as the Woman, the grown daughter of Carrie, 20 years in the future.

All characters wear appropriate street clothes. The action begins in spring, continues into summer.

Setting

The play is set mainly in Carrie's working-class living-room. We recommend a minimal setting on an open stage, with no attempt at realistic doors and walls.

In some performances, the Hacker appeared initially sitting within the audience or at a side aisle. Bringing him into the auditorium can be very effective. The producer should feel free to adapt the staging to the available resources.

Notes

In 1993, The Franklin Institute, Philadelphia's major science museum, mounted a national touring exhibit on AIDS. While focusing on scientific aspects, it also included moving testimonies of persons with AIDS. But the exhibit designers felt that more was needed to give visitors — especially teenagers — a strong personal stake in assimilating facts. So we were asked to create a play for school groups attending the exhibit.

Could we create a piece that sidestepped the politics and preachments about AIDS and spoke to each viewer directly, despite audience diversity — middle and upper school, inner city and suburban, the very conservative and the sexually active? Issue-driven plays tend to be one-dimensional, while in real life, issues aren't born shrink-wrapped and labeled. So our play evolved as a play not solely about AIDS but about *risk, honesty and trust in any relationship*. Its root message: "Use your head. Communicate. This means you."

After its three-month run at The Franklin Institute, the play was produced by other museums and schools around the USA; and The Independent Eye staged its own touring version.

In our race-conscious society, casting is never "color-blind" — every combination has connotations. But we suggest multiracial casting where talent permits. At Franklin Institute, the actors playing Carrie and Gil were African-American, the Hacker and Joy were Caucasian. Sometimes a Latino played Gil or a Caucasian played Carrie. The one essential for the actors is an ease in addressing the audience directly. The questions within the play draw the audience into personal connection, but only if the actors really *ask* the questions rather than "act" asking the questions — no protective barrier.

The play can be performed simply as a play. For us, though, a play is always a stimulus to thought about human behavior. So we encourage post-show discussion about the content. If that happens, it's desirable to have someone on hand with formal training as an AIDS educator. But a post-play discussion is not an expert telling the audience what to think; instead, it must start with the specifics of the play and harness energy into channels that, in this real world, produce hope and positive action. After the text of the play, we've outlined the discussion strategy we've used for *A Friend from High School.* This structure can be adapted to the other plays in this volume.

Why is the Hacker called the Hacker? To us, a personified virus is most akin to a computer hacker whose sense of ethics is non-existent. He doesn't think of himself as evil; he simply has a sense of delight in his uncanny power to make big things happen. He can be played broadly, but he's not Dracula.

Is this play still relevant, given news of new drug treatments for AIDS? In the minds of many, we've "cured" it. Apart from the limitations of current treatments — different effects on different individuals, and the drugs' enormous cost making them unaffordable for most — there's the simple fact that other venereal diseases have been "cured" for decades, yet still are rampant and enormously damaging. We have not yet found a cure for dishonesty and ignorance: that's what the play is about.

A Friend from High School

Lights. A young woman, about 19, wearing glasses, appears, reading a diary as she comes downstage. She looks up at us, then sits on the floor and finishes reading a passage. At last, she speaks to us:

WOMAN

Did you ever think how you came to be born? What your mom and dad were thinking about? My mom, what she told me. . .

Think of your best friend. Think. What if they died? Or no, you don't want to have bad dreams. But how about the one person you really don't like. Somebody you really hate. They're dumb. Or smell bad. Or maybe the other way: they're too smart. Too popular. Just too much. Think about that kid.

What if *they* died? If they died the worst way anybody could die? How many of you would really like to see'em die?

Starts to raise her own hand, stops.

No. I guess not. Maybe a bad headache. Or an itch. But not die.

Suddenly, the Hacker stands up in the auditorium. He's dressed in suit, tie, fedora, sunglasses. High energy, not a hint of malevolence, just enthusiasm.

HACKER

Friends, guys, young ladies, I know why you're here. You're checking out a disease, right? Modern, state of the art. It's a terrific disease, you can really have fun catching it, and nobody's gonna screw it up by curing you, cause there is no cure. I mean why go to the trouble of vomiting and diarrhea and hideous pain if then you recover? Sure, you've read about miracle drugs, but they don't *cure* anything, even if you can pay those big, big bucks. We can still guarantee there's a very good chance that you will die.

WOMAN

Stop! You don't belong here! Please go!

HACKER *(cheerfully)*

I'll wait.

WOMAN

He's always hanging around.

He walks away. She waits a moment, continues, to us. As she speaks, he drifts back.

I want to tell you about my mother. Her name is Carrie. She couldn't be here cause she works. She's a nurse. I'll be her.

She had a worst enemy. And a best friend. They both died. They were the same person.

Walks into the center.

We're going way back in time. To 1999. How many of you were born in 1999?

Encourages a show of hands.

1999? That's nineteen years ago. That's when I was born.

Hacker reappears in the same place.

HACKER

Now?

WOMAN

Get lost!

HACKER

I'll wait.

He disappears again.

WOMAN

Now I'll be my mother.

She takes off her glasses. Now's she's Carrie. A young man — Gil — appears, hugs her from behind.

CARRIE

I'm nineteen, about to be twenty, and I just found out that. . . *(turning to Gil)* Gil . . . I'm pregnant.

GIL

You're what? *(pause)* How'd that happen?

CARRIE

Gil, you were there at the time!

GIL

Does your mother know?

She crosses to the couch, sits. Gil sits beside her, tries to comfort her.

CARRIE

Yeh. She just says, "Well, marry the dummy." Gil, I'm gonna keep the baby, I know that much and that's all I know, cause if we already bought the ticket, we're gonna ride the train—

GIL
Ok, I—

CARRIE
And if you're gonna give me a big thing about "Well how do I know I'm the father?" then you just turn around and take your butt right out of here—

GIL
Whatta you yelling at me?— Ok. Fine. Sure. Hey, you know how I feel—

CARRIE
I don't know how you feel!

GIL
Just gimme a chance!

CARRIE
Stop yelling at me!

GIL
You wanta get married, fine!

CARRIE
Married! You think I want to marry you?

GIL
Don't you?

CARRIE *(in agony)*
Yes!

Embraces him. Then pulls away.

GIL
But hey, how did we— I thought you were always careful.

CARRIE
Me? We!

GIL
Ok, "we."

CARRIE
Except when you got in one of your cave-man moods.

She tries to regain control.

I just think we might have communicated better. I mean like talk.

GIL
Talk. What's to talk?

CARRIE
I keep messing up. The one thing I said— I'm not gonna be like my mom. Kids. Dead end job. Tired all the time—

GIL

Hey—

She goes up to the table above the couch, sorts a basket of unsorted socks as she collects herself.

CARRIE

I was gonna work a while, make some money, try to save money by moving back home to Mom, and then I can go to modeling school—

GIL

We'll be ok—

CARRIE

People say "You look like a model." Yeh, right. *(indicating her shape)* I'll be out to here.

GIL

We'll be ok—

CARRIE

I always set myself up. "Oh this one time it doesn't matter." And I'm saving for school, and suddenly we're gonna have hospital bills—

GIL

We'll be ok—

CARRIE

Great way to start a family. We never talked about the future. Now we're right square into it.

GIL

You better start taking the Pill.

CARRIE

Don't you think it's kinda late for that?

The actor playing the Hacker has gone backstage, calls to her, as her brother:

VOICE *(off)*

Carrie! Mom says finish the dishes, and there's a phone call. Pick it up.

CARRIE *(to Gil)*

Hold on. I'm not finished—

She picks up phone. At a distance, Joy appears, holding a cordless phone. As they speak, Gil continues remonstrating with Carrie.

Hi?

JOY
Hi Carrie. This is Joy. You remember me from high school?

CARRIE
What?

JOY
Joy, from high school.

CARRIE
Oh.

JOY
Did I catch you at a bad time?

CARRIE
Yes.

GIL
Listen to me!

JOY
Listen, this is very weird, me calling you out of the blue, but I have to meet with you, it's very important—

CARRIE
What? What for?

GIL
I'm talking to you!

JOY
I can't talk on the phone, but is there some time tomorrow?

CARRIE
I work till 5:30.

JOY
Can I come there?

GIL
Damn it, hang up the phone!

Gil tries to embrace Carrie. She shoves him away.

CARRIE
What? Yeh— Yeh, 622 Franklin.

JOY
Great. Six o'clock.

CARRIE
Ok. Bye.

Hangs up.

What does *she* want?

GIL

Who?

CARRIE

My least favorite person in high school. Not a friend. Definitely not a friend. So damn smart and pretty and popular it made you wanta puke. *(to Gil, impulsively)* Would you please *go*!

GIL *(exasperated)*

What is it? You want me to stay or want me to go?

CARRIE

Yes! No! Both!

Carrie rushes to Gil, embraces him.

GIL

Carrie, look, we'll be ok. I'll take care of everything.

CARRIE

Like you took care of this.

GIL

Give me a smile.

CARRIE

Huh?

GIL

Little smile for me? One little smile?

She stops, then gives him a broad, leering grimace. He shrugs, goes out. Carrie turns to us.

CARRIE

Well you're looking at me. How many of you think I did something wrong, or immoral, or just plain stupid?

Encourages a show of hands.

Ok, maybe. Well am I the only one? How many of you, some time, thought you could get across the street ok and almost got hit by a car?

Hands.

How many ever took a risk that could have got you hurt, or changed your life some way that you wouldn't like?

Hands.

Me too.

VOICE *(off)*

Carrie, your friend's here!

CARRIE

What friend?

Joy appears.

JOY

Me.

Carrie sees her. Suddenly, the Hacker appears, saunters down to talk to us:

HACKER

I think it's time we get in some educational material here, cause if we don't get it in right away, you won't have time to forget it.

See, the best thing about this disease, it can be with you for years and you never notice. It's the gift that keeps on giving. Give it to all your friends. Something to remember you by.

JOY & CARRIE

Out!

He shrugs, goes off. They turn toward each other.

JOY

Were you busy?

Carrie suppresses her anger, goes to pick up the basket, then sits, sorting the socks, avoiding Joy.

CARRIE

No, just finishing the laundry. My brother can't sort his own socks.

JOY

How have you been?

CARRIE

Ok. I've been working. Live here with my mom, try to save money to go to school. I might be getting married.

JOY

That's great. Yeh. Wow. Well, I've been going to school. Villanova.

Joy hesitates, then sits beside her. Carrie continues sorting socks.

CARRIE

You always did good.

JOY

I had to drop out. I've been sick.

Pause.

Well I know it's awkward and it seems strange to you that I called, but. . .

CARRIE
So whatja want?

JOY
I wanted to talk to you because, a guy I dated for a while. . . You remember Ric?

CARRIE
Ric?

JOY
You were going with him for a while.

CARRIE
Last time I heard of him, he put together another band and they ran off with his car.

JOY
Yeh, well, I talked to him a couple weeks ago, actually, and— This is pretty awkward. I have reasons for asking you about Ric. How serious were you about Ric, do you mind my asking you this?

CARRIE
"Serious?" Whatta you mean "serious"?

JOY
Did you have sex with him?

CARRIE *(outraged)*
What?!?

JOY
Well you know what HIV means, don't you? AIDS?

Carrie rises, spilling the socks. Then gathers them up furiously and carries the basket up to the table.

CARRIE
Oh God, I'm so sick of hearing about that stuff. Those people, it's their own fault. All that garbage. I got my own problems.

Pause.

Has Ric got AIDS?

JOY
He said he didn't. I don't know. I can't say. I asked him. He said no.

Pause.

He was really messed up. He was into drugs. That made him kind of exotic, I guess. I mean here I was this nice girl, blonde, honor roll, drama club, and this guy—

Joy rises, approaches Carrie.

But I'm trying to contact anybody that might have been with Ric— I mean doing anything that— Just to say that it'd be a good idea if they got a test for HIV, if they had any reason to think—

CARRIE

I don't really know what you're talking about. I'm feeling fine.

JOY

I don't know how to say this, I'm not trying to scare you, or make you panic, but I'm HIV-positive. In fact I've been in the hospital three times—

CARRIE

That's your problem.

Hacker, overjoyed, emerges from the wings, comes between Carrie and Joy, puts his arm around the frozen Joy.

HACKER

That's what we like to hear. "It's her problem." Terrific. Right, you just went with this guy a while when you were a sophomore, and it made you feel grownup, sure. But you didn't do anything weird. You have to do something real weird to get AIDS, right?

CARRIE

Who are you?

HACKER

I'm the star of the show.

CARRIE

What's your name?

JOY

HIV.

Hacker shakes Carrie's hand. She recoils.

HACKER

Hey. Don't worry. Handshakes aren't what I'm about. We have to get better acquainted than that. My friend here. She knows me very well.

He holds the pose a moment, then sharply breaks it, comes down as the others move away: Joy off, Carrie down to the corner where she began.

This is a great play. I'm gonna watch. See what happens.

Gil appears, comes down to the Hacker.

GIL
What is it?

HACKER
It's a play about AIDS.

GIL *(clowning)*
Gaahrgh! I've got AIDS!

HACKER
Hey, cool it. This is educational.

Carrie puts on glasses, speaks to us as the daughter in the future.

WOMAN
My mom was really scared. I mean come on, she hadn't even *liked* the guy. You're not supposed to get punished for something you don't enjoy. But next time she had her appointment at the clinic, she heard herself saying—

Her mouth moves, speaking inaudibly, as Joy's voice speaks the words.

VOICE
Maybe you should test me for HIV.

WOMAN
It took two weeks to get the test results. How many of you like to take tests, any kind of tests?

Hands.

How many really hate it?

Hands.

How many remember some time when you were really worried about your grade?

Hands.

How many really understand what it is she's worried about?

Hacker jumps up, full of naive enthusiasm.

HACKER
Well it's so neat the way it works. Ok, this is not a flashy disease where you break out in spots and turn green. And it's hard to catch. But look on the bright side. It lays back there five years, ten years, before you have any idea you've got it, and so think about all that extra time you've got to give it to your friends.

GIL *(confused)*

Hey, but—

HACKER

And since you have to actually *do* something to catch it, everyone will say it's your own fault, and they'll never imagine they could get it.

GIL

But—

HACKER

And you get more for your money. Why come down with a disease that just does one thing? With me, we get right to the heart of the immune system, so you can die twenty or thirty different ways. A consumer's paradise. It's a terrific disease.

Looks to the Woman.

Carry on.

WOMAN

My mother said it was the worst two weeks of her life. For two weeks, she had nightmares. She dreamed about her wedding.

She takes off her glasses. Gil crosses to her, offers his arm. Joy enters as the Pastor, wearing a surgical mask and lab coat. The Hacker drapes his arms over Carrie's shoulders, letting his weight drag her down. Gil and Carrie walk in slow motion toward the Pastor, dragging the Hacker along behind. All hum "The Wedding March."

Note: This sequence is played as a comic horror-show, rife with movie cliches. The actors move and speak in slow motion. But within this farcical style, Carrie's terror is real.

GIL

You look tired.

CARRIE

I've got a lot on my mind.

GIL

Who's that?

CARRIE

Just a guy.

Joy confronts them as the Pastor.

JOY

Do you take each other?

CARRIE & GIL

We do.

HACKER

So do I.

He grabs their shoulders abruptly. They scream, rush to sit on the couch, as if in bed. Hacker ensconces himself between them.

GIL

Could we have a little privacy here?

HACKER

Don't mind me.

Joy comes behind the couch, putting surgical masks and oven mitts on Carrie and Gil.

JOY

Can't be too careful.

They try to kiss, reaching across the Hacker.

CARRIE

This isn't my idea of a real hot time.

Joy dumps a basketful of her brother's mismatched socks into her lap.

JOY

Always practice Safe Sox.

Hacker momentarily comes to life:

HACKER

Safe Sox. I love jokes like that. They kill me. They kill you.

Carrie frantically sorts socks, looking for something.

GIL

Carrie? Baby? I'm here.

CARRIE

Two weeks.

GIL

Hey, let's just be together.

CARRIE

Two weeks.

GIL

We've got our whole lives.

CARRIE

Two weeks.

GIL
This isn't fair.

CARRIE
It isn't fair. I stopped smoking. I'm taking vitamins. That was clear back in high school. That doesn't count.

GIL
That doesn't count. That's before we knew each other.

CARRIE
We still don't. We were able to make a baby without knowing a thing about each other.

She suddenly holds up a pair of infant's booties.

What's this?

GIL
Our baby.

Hacker grabs the socks.

HACKER
Mine!

Carrie shrieks, rises abruptly. Freeze.

HACKER
That got her.

Hacker comes down, talks to us.

Hey. Does she have anything to worry about? How much do you know about this? How many think she *could* have HIV?

Hands.

How many think she could get it from shaking hands with Joy?

Hands.

How many think it's just something they made up to scare people. It doesn't exist.

Hands.

How many think that if you're gonna die you're gonna die, so it doesn't matter what you do?

Hands.

You're my kinda people. We don't want to mess up your chances. Those three guys asleep in the back row? Couple girls giggling down there? You work at it, you can stay dumb, and in a few years we'll get to know each other pretty well.

Hacker goes off. Phone rings. Carrie rushes on to answer it. Joy, appears as a Nurse, with phone receiver.

NURSE

The doctor asked me to let you know that it's good news. The test results are negative.

CARRIE

Ok. . .

NURSE

But if you have reason to believe your baby's father might be at risk, he should be tested.

CARRIE

I don't know what reason there'd be to think he had a problem.

NURSE

Whatever reason you had to think that *you* might have a problem.

Pause.

CARRIE

Ok. Thanks.

Hangs up, turns as Gil appears.

So?

He's incredulous at the request she's just made:

GIL

Are you kidding?

CARRIE

I got tested.

GIL

So that settles it. No problem.

CARRIE

Gil, I didn't think there was any reason for me. The thing with that guy was years and years ago.

GIL

Let's get a pizza.

CARRIE

Are you telling me that I was your one and only? That you were totally inexperienced?

GIL

No. Hey, you think I'm gay or something? I'm not gay.

CARRIE
Well goodie for you. Didn't you tell me that you slept with other people?

GIL
They didn't have AIDS.

CARRIE
How do you know that?

GIL
Ok, I had girlfriends, sure. That's in the past. You have to trust.

CARRIE
I trusted one guy.

GIL
He was different.

CARRIE
But you're ok.

GIL
Don't you believe me?

CARRIE
I believe you think you're ok. But I don't think you have the foggiest idea.

Gil is at the breaking point, saying the first thing that comes into his head:

GIL
Look, maybe it sounds bad to say, but you know and I know that AIDS is getting rid of lots of people that nobody will ever miss!

CARRIE
Like Joy.

GIL
Well you said you hated her. You said—

Silence.

I don't want to talk about the past. What's past is done with. If you trust me, you trust me.

He goes out. Carrie sits on the sofa, angry and depressed.

CARRIE
I don't think *any* of these socks match.

She speaks to us:

I couldn't stop being mad. It was all her fault. Joy. Getting me panicked. Blow-up with Gil. It made me so mad. I'm gonna tell her—

Impulsively, she phones Joy to tell her off. Hacker appears in auditorium, with phone receiver.

HACKER

Oh hi. Sorry, Joy's in the hospital. With any luck she's probably going to die. How about a date?

Carrie hangs up. Hacker disappears. Gil appears, speaks to us:

GIL

I didn't call Carrie for three days. I was so mad. She doesn't trust me. How do you take a test for trust? We made a baby together. How much more *together* can we be? We know each other by now, don't we?

Hacker appears, beside him.

HACKER

Don't you think you're kinda ridiculous? Letting her run all over you. She's pregnant. So what? Is that your fault? What would your friends say? They'd laugh at you. You got a right to your own life. Show her who's boss. Be a man. Dump her. *(to audience)* Am I right?

GIL

Don't bother me. Get outa here.

HACKER

Be that way. Insult me. Abuse me. I'm still your friend.

Hacker backs off. Gil turns, watches as Joy and Carrie appear, shopping.

JOY

When you have to get back?

CARRIE

I work two to ten.

JOY

Wow.

CARRIE

I like mornings. I'm glad you called. I been thinking about going out shopping. Oh look at those shoes!

JOY

They're so tiny!

CARRIE
I don't even know what size babies are sposed to be.

Pause.

Joy, thanks for calling me. I tried to call, you were in the hospital, and I didn't know. . . You don't look sick. You look fine.

JOY
I'm not real fine. I take about twenty pills a day. At least I haven't lost my appetite. I run round with pills in one hand and a sandwich in the other. But I get— Well how do *you* feel? You feel the baby?

CARRIE
Sometimes I think I do. Kind of a flutter? I'm sposed to feel happy, but mostly I'm scared to death.

JOY
Gil seems like a good guy. I mean a lotta guys—

CARRIE
Yeh, *most* guys, I know, they'd say, "Hey, it's your problem, honey." But I think, how much do I really know this guy? Do I know him well enough for *this?* You ok?

JOY
Kinda tired. Oh look at these!

CARRIE *(pointing at imaginary item)*
Little overalls.

JOY
My mom still has mine. My "Oshkosh suit."

CARRIE
You live at your parents'?

JOY
My mom lost my dad two years ago, so my getting sick was really hard on her. When I found out, I didn't even *move* for about three weeks. And people say, "No, it's not a death sentence, there are people who survive a long time," but—
But, then I thought, well I can't just keep lying here, it's boring. Get some air in my tires. So I thought about you and—

Pause. She starts to break down, then recovers.

It hit me. You're having a baby, and you're not ready for it, and I'll never have one, ready or not. Shouldn't get emotional in a department store.

Carrie takes hold of Joy's arm. She gathers strength. They go out. Hacker sidles in.

GIL *(to us)*
So all of a sudden she's spending a whole lot of time with this girlfriend, Joy. Going to a movie. Hey, why is she going to a movie with her? She's supposed to spend her time with me.

HACKER
She seems closer to Joy than to you, right?

GIL
Yeh. Here she's talking to her, and she's not talking to me, or just telling me what they talked about.

HACKER
Maybe you weren't all that close.

GIL
Maybe.

HACKER
Lot easier to make a baby than to talk. I mean talk about anything personal.

GIL
A lot.

HACKER
She better watch out. She might catch AIDS from her, right? *(to audience)* Am I right?

GIL
Will you shut up!

HACKER
Glad to.

Disappears. Gil comes into the living room.

GIL *(calling)*
Carrie!

CARRIE *(appearing)*
What?

GIL
You better be careful. Like with Joy. I mean think of the baby. You might touch her and—

CARRIE
Don't be silly. That's not how you get AIDS.

GIL
Ok, I know technically. But you never know.

It's the last straw. Carrie loses her temper:

CARRIE
Look dummy, be real! If you think you can spread it by talking, or touching, or sneezing, then you don't know enough about it to avoid catching it! Dummy!

Carrie goes out. Gil stands, nearly speechless.

GIL
"Dummy." She called me "dummy." I don't call that communication.

He goes to his corner, sulking, watches Carrie and Joy enter, with cokes and a bowl of popcorn. Joy carries a shopping bag. They sit on the sofa.

JOY
This is like high school! I miss it.

CARRIE
I don't. I hated it.

JOY
I loved it. Everything was safe then.

CARRIE
Safe? *(laughing)* You was in a different *world*, honey.

JOY
I guess. Maybe that's why I was so crazy about Ric. Somebody that wasn't *safe*. I couldn't believe that I was fifteen and dating a senior with a car.

CARRIE
And who shot up.

JOY
Oh yeh, I thought, wow, he's living right on the edge. He's taking risks. He stood me up, he stole money from me—

CARRIE
Once he hit me—

JOY
And the scarier he was, the more exciting. I wasn't ready for it, Carrie. Any of it.

CARRIE
He say, "Oh you want it, baby!" And yeh, but wanting to fly and being *ready* to fly are not the same. I thought I was ready, and I wasn't ready. Even with Gil I wasn't ready. You have to be able to talk. And listen.

JOY
I have to take my pills.

Takes a pill box out of her purse.

CARRIE
What is all that?

JOY
Well, this is my main medicine. And this is supposed to counteract the side effects of my main medicine. This is a vitamin supplement. More side effects. This I think the doctor just gave me cause I like the color red.

Takes pills, washes them down with coke. More.

I don't like this a whole lot.

CARRIE
Did you call him? Ric? I mean about this?

JOY
Yeh. He's down in Wilmington. Bartending. He says he's feeling fine. I don't believe him. He sounded scared.

Pause.

Carrie, I always wondered. . . This is kinda personal, but. . . I remember a lot about the back seat of his car. But I don't remember much about feeling anything. Was he any good?

CARRIE *(laughing)*
Joy! I think he had so many girls because he kept trying to get it right. He was all smoke and no fire.

They laugh.

All alarms and no firetruck!

Laughter. Then they grow quiet.

JOY
Carrie, I asked my mom if I could give you this. For the baby.

Digs in the shopping bag, takes out a bundle: a pair of toddler's overalls.

It was mine.

CARRIE
Thanks.

They look at one another, overcome with emotion.

Let's listen to some music.

They get up, go out. Gil turns away.

HACKER
Still mad, huh?

No response.

This is what you get for being a responsible guy. She called you Dummy. Teach her some respect. Hit her.

Gil glares at him.

Cause don't you hate people who tell you the truth and talk sense and know all the facts and use their brains? Who do they think they are?

GIL
She's right.

HACKER
Huh?

GIL
She's right. Carrie's right. I'm gonna get the damn test.

HACKER
Hey, suppose you find out something you don't want to know?

GIL *(angrier)*
I don't want to give a disease to somebody I love!

HACKER
If they get it they deserve it.

GIL *(enraged)*
I'm gonna—!

HACKER
Bash my head in? Surprise! I don't have a head, I'm a virus. Sub-microscopic. You can't kill me. You can only prevent me.

GIL
Then I will *prevent* your butt right outa here.

Chases him across the stage and off. Then he controls himself, takes a breath, and calls:

Carrie!

She appears.

Ok. I got the damned test. No problem. I'm clean. Satisfied?

CARRIE
Thank you, Gil.

GIL
Nothing wrong.

CARRIE

Great.

GIL

I told you that.

CARRIE

Good.

GIL

And it really makes me mad. The thing that really makes me mad— You were jerking me around, and yelling and screaming at me, and call me Dummy, and ok, but the thing that really makes me mad is—

You were right. I know it coulda been different. I knew I wasn't honest. I saw right through me.

Carrie embraces him. Hacker appears.

HACKER

Guys, good for you. You're healthy, you're happy. But there's still time. Keep in mind: the world is coming to an end. Epidemics. Toxic waste. Drive-by shootings. You could die tomorrow. So there's no reason to plan for the future. There *is* no future. So just do whatever you want to do. Just do it.

CARRIE & GIL

Out!

Hacker shrugs, goes. Joy appears with a duffel bag, starts packing clothing. Gil watches.

CARRIE

When are you leaving?

JOY

Eight in the morning. Which means my mom will be ready to go at six. Oh it's so gorgeous up there—

CARRIE

I never been to Cape Cod. We went to Ocean City once.

JOY

Beaches, water, air. We were going last month, and then I got sick again.

CARRIE

You look a lot better.

JOY

I feel better. My mom and I really wanted some private time before—

CARRIE
I'll miss you.

JOY
It's only two weeks. Maybe I can feel the baby move by then.

CARRIE
Gil can't wait. I think he feels one kick he'll drop dead. I was going to get you this sun hat. Big straw brim, with a Coca Cola can wired onto one side, and the other side says, "Let's Party."

JOY
You wanta fold these?

Pause.

Is Gil still mad you're coming over here.

CARRIE
He's real funny. No. No, I think we're both growing up real fast. I get so scared. I'm not ready for this. Run into these girls I knew from high school. Three kids before they're twenty, and on welfare, and no man, and fat as a hippopotamus—
If I get through this— I mean my idea of modeling school is out the window, I'm not going to take a gamble on something like that, and Gil says he wants to go back to school, but what if he gets laid off— I am not ready!

Pause. With grim humor:

Well so I guess I'll *get* ready. It could have been worse.

Carrie looks at her, realizes what she's said.

I'm sorry.

JOY
Right. It could have been worse.

CARRIE
Joy, what do you want?

JOY
What?

CARRIE
What do you want for the future?

JOY
Well, next week we'll be in Cape Cod. That's as far as I look ahead.

CARRIE
But when you get better?

JOY
Well, Carrie, hey. I won't.

CARRIE
You will.

JOY
What I want?

Joy stops packing. Long silence. Joy's cheerful control suddenly breaks. She turns front, to us, speaks with all the rage she's withheld:

What I want. One night's sleep when I don't break out in sweat. Go out running like I used to. Stop the damn itching. Get my fingers to coordinate. Wake up rested. Have somebody that's not afraid to hold me and kiss me. Be able to think some day about having children. Stop hearing my mom cry. Stop taking pills. Stop hurting. Stop waking up in the morning and thinking it's just a dream and remembering it isn't a dream, it's real!

Her rage spent, she pauses, speaks to us:

That's what I wanted to say. But I didn't say it.

Turns to Carrie.

Well. . . I think mostly what I'm gonna do next week.

GIL
Carrie said that she realized that she'd never hugged her. She didn't know what to do.

Joy takes Carrie's hand, speaks quietly.

JOY
Carrie, I wish I could be as bouncy and bubbly and funny as I was in high school. If we'd been friends then, you'd have a more entertaining friend. I look in the mirror now and I really depress myself: "What a wimp!" But this is me. This is your friend from high school.

GIL *(to us)*
Would you have? How many would actually put out your arms and hug a friend with AIDS?

Hands.

And how many think, however you feel about it, that you probably would not?

He watches us raise our hands, or not. Then he turns to watch. Carrie embraces Joy.

Hacker appears behind them, holding an alarm clock. The alarm goes off. Joy starts to go. Halts, gives Carrie a letter. Then she leaves.

GIL

Carrie didn't see Joy again. Joy was at the beach, came down with pneumonia, went to the hospital, bunch of complications, and very suddenly died. Carrie got a letter.

Carrie opens the letter, reads it.

CARRIE

Joy. . .

Gil embraces her. When the embrace is complete, both move apart, Gil offstage. Carrie comes forward, puts on glasses as the daughter.

WOMAN *(to us)*

My mother married my dad, and they're still together. They had another kid, my brother, little snot. And my mom, she never got to be a model, and she did get kinda fat, but she went back to school, and she's a nurse.

And my dad, they fight a lot, and she still calls him Dummy. But they are very, very honest. That's what keeps them together.

She picks up the toddler's overalls from the sofa. Then sees the Hacker at a distance.

He's still around. He's going to hang around a long time. Some people thought there'd be a miracle cure, and others thought we'd all die. But it's like everything else. You can't depend on miracles, and you can't depend on disaster. Just have to muddle through. But there is a future. We'll survive.

Looks at the overalls she holds.

My mother named me Joy.

Lights fade.

The Discussion

After the curtain call, the actors come forward, sit on the edge of the stage, introduce themselves, and start with questions requiring only a show of hands, to break the ice.

> Hi. I'm Sally. That's Jack, Amy, Brian. I'd like to ask you some questions.
>
> How many of you are under sixteen? *(Hands)* And how many sixteen or older?
>
> How many of you are living with both of your birth parents? Both your mom and your dad? *(Hands)* And how many otherwise?

We begin with these simple "show of hands" questions as a means of getting an interaction started. Other questions can be used, but they should be questions that everyone can answer, suggesting that we're not only talking about a "case history," but about our own lives. We continue with more personal questions. It's important that discussion leaders raise their own hands in response: the subject concerns all of us, not just those "at risk."

> How many think that if you had a problem, you could talk to your mom or dad — or whoever you live with — no matter what it was? Anything at all?
>
> And how may feel there are some things you definitely would not talk about?
>
> How many of you have had somebody who was close to you die?
>
> How many have actually seen someone die? Not on TV — but actually been there and seen someone die?

The transition between yes/no hand-raising and actual audience dialogue is easy with some groups, difficult with others. We try to find a question that allows simple answers of a word or a phrase, centered not in intellectual but in emotional response to the play. No answer is wrong. Keep the focus on the actual question; don't let it wander off.

> How did this guy (the Hacker) make you feel?

Then, when people are participating fully, go on to the next.

> There's a lot in the play about taking risks. What kinds of risks do the characters in the play take?

Most will start with the obvious: Joy and Carrie had unsafe sex. But this is not only about literal risk but also emotional risk. If someone says, "Carrie took a risk in hugging Joy," that's not scientifically true, but for that character, it felt like a risk.

Each character takes risks. For Joy: risking Carrie's hostility in the first contact; later, a fear of rejection; the emotional investment in fighting AIDS rather than giving up. For Carrie: the risk of having sex when she knew she wasn't ready; of keeping the baby; of getting the test and facing the possibilities; of rejection by Gil; of being close to someone in need. For Gil: the risk of taking responsibility; of ridicule from buddies; of admitting he's wrong, perhaps losing her respect.

Whether or not the discussion includes a straight question-and-answer phase, it should include a way for the audience to get answers to questions they're unable or unwilling to ask in the public space.

> Let's go back to the play for a minute. What do you think the characters learned? How did they change?

It's important that the audience feel they've made a real contribution, that they've been not only recipients but gift-givers. If they haven't contributed to your own thinking, then re-examine your techniques for the next time. One-way transactions are, by definition, dead. It's useful to summarize points that have struck you as illuminating and to have a prepared conclusion so that it doesn't seem to trail off — perhaps a brief personal response from each actor to the characters and the play.

Get Happy

Characters

Cheryl, a high school student
Luann, her close friend
Mother of Cheryl
Kim, Cheryl's younger sister
Father of Cheryl
Nick, her cousin, in his early twenties
Brian, Cheryl's boyfriend
Kenny, Luann's boyfriend

If desired, the play can be performed by four women and two men, with the Father and Nick doubling as Brian and Kenny. The full cast is preferable.

Setting

A bare stage, with chairs set in three separate areas as a living room, a rec room, and an automobile. A chair is at one side. While it's possible to do a more complete visual setting, it should be kept as simple as possible, in keeping with the play's straightforward story-telling style.

Notes

This play, based on improvisations by a high school workshop, centers on the issue of teenage alcohol abuse. But a play shouldn't be approached with a focus on its "issue." Our play *Dessie* was presented cross-country for hundreds of showings because it happened to coincide with a time at which child abuse became a hot headline topic. We had created it as a response to the pervasive violence in American working-class life, a sense of people as disposable commodities. The tendency of sponsors to focus on the narrow issue of child abuse made it easier to sell but hard to avoid a sense, in post-show discussions, that child abuse was a sort of exotic disease separate from other social ills.

So in directing this workshop, we focused on actions that had little direct relation to getting drunk and smashing up a car. Nor did we use such catch-phrases as "peer pressure" or "positive self-image." We started with questions very close to home: What experience have you had where you felt really trapped? What did somebody say to you that really hurt? What do you dislike most about the person you love the most? And so on. We did our best to avoid the generalities that lie over most "problem plays" like melted cheese. We recommend the same approach in producing *Get Happy*. The tragic outcome rises from many small interactions that seem insignificant but which add up. Making each moment real is the only way to reach an understanding that goes beyond the obvious.

We have avoided the usual practice of acting editions, appending prop lists, clothing descriptions and detailed stage directions, as if a play were merely a lifelike TV dinner. What the person wears, what's littering the dinner table, what's in pockets or purse — these want the very particular, immediate choices that real people make every day. In the text, we don't give Cheryl's Father a name; but the actor himself should give him a name and should base his clothing, his mannerisms, and his pathetic attempts at coping not on comic stereotypes but on Real Fathers He Has Known. The poor man is making himself into a stereotype by his frustration, but none of us were born that way. There are no villains here. Every character winds up, as do we all at some time or another, doing the wrong thing at the wrong time. Yes, it might have helped Cheryl to have a different father, a different cousin, or a different boyfriend; but life doesn't deal everybody four aces.

Because the play doesn't have an easy moral tag, it may be programmed with a post-show discussion. We recommend this in an instructional context. But we suggest that any discussion start from concrete questions, not from a recital of generalities. The play is only one story, intended to provoke questions about choices and behavior. What, in fact, could the parents do, faced with a flat lie? What would you do for Cheryl if you were Nick or Luann? Why wasn't she able to open up to Nick or to speak to a counselor? How do you relate to a friend after a tragedy? What do you have in common with these people? That's the starting-point for the cast as well as for the audience.

Get Happy

Bare stage except for three groups of chairs in areas separated from one another. Another chair, far right, faced upstage.

Pop music, faint. Characters appear in distant areas of the stage, standing or sitting. During scenes they're not involved in, they may remain in these positions, focused in the direction of the scene.

Cheryl comes forward to an area at the far left. Luann moves to the right chair, looking at Cheryl.

LUANN

Cheryl was my best friend. Since we were little kids. She still is, far as I'm concerned. I just wish she'd talk to me.

Luann turns and watches. Cheryl goes off. Two others enter the area set as a living room.

Mother at table, opening a stack of mail. Small girl, Kim, on floor doing homework.

MOTHER

Wow, two days away and the mail piles up.

KIM

I hate this math. Mrs. Leonard is such a zombie.

MOTHER

How was your weekend, hon?

KIM

I did some of the dishes.

MOTHER

Need some help?

KIM

I need a calculator.

MOTHER

It's so nice to be able to go away with your father and have some fun, and know we've got two kids we can trust, and come back and all the dishes are clean, almost. What's this?

Picks up a piece of broken pottery.

KIM

Piece of something.

MOTHER
Did you and Cheryl get along ok? No fights?

KIM
She's kinda bossy.

MOTHER
Well we told you when we're gone she's in charge.

KIM
She made me supper. Hot dogs. And breakfast too.

MOTHER
That's great.

KIM
Froot Loops. She put too much milk in it.

MOTHER
Well you survived. Wonder what is this—?

KIM
It's that ugly looking vase you had in the den.

MOTHER *(correcting her automatically)*
Vah-z.

KIM
Vah-z.

MOTHER
Who broke it?

KIM
Maybe Cheryl's friends.

MOTHER
When?

KIM
Saturday night.

MOTHER
Did Cheryl have friends over here Saturday night?

KIM
I dunno. *(pause)* Maybe.

MOTHER
Did she or didn't she?

KIM
No. Except . . . just some of her friends. But she didn't want you to worry so she told me not to tell.

FATHER *(off)*
We're home!

MOTHER
Who was here?

KIM
Just Brian, and some others, but they weren't here very long.

Father enters, tossing his coat over a chair.

FATHER
Cheryl's not feeling good, so I took her to work, but then brought her right home.

KIM
She'd barf on the Big Macs.

MOTHER
Would you call her in here?

FATHER
She's up in her room—

MOTHER
They had a party here last night.

KIM
No, Mom—

MOTHER *(calling)*
Cheryl!

CHERYL *(off)*
What?

MOTHER
Come here.

CHERYL *(off)*
I'm not feeling good.

MOTHER
Right now.

FATHER
Now take it easy.

MOTHER
She was supposed to watch Kim. She was not supposed to have friends over. They broke our vase.

FATHER
Ok—

Cheryl enters, in a bathrobe. Stands at entryway.

CHERYL
I'm not feeling good. I'm gonna rest.

MOTHER
You didn't sleep too well?

CHERYL
Uh-uh.

MOTHER
How late were you up?

CHERYL
Not real late.

MOTHER
What time did your friends leave?

KIM *(defending her sister)*
Mom, it wasn't a party, cause Cheryl was gone all evening and they didn't come back here till after Doctor Doom was on.

CHERYL
What friends?

MOTHER
Your friends who were here.

CHERYL
I didn't have any friends here.

FATHER
Wait a minute—

KIM
She didn't, Mom. They just came in, she couldn't help it—

MOTHER
We told you to take care of Kim—

KIM
She did. She made me go to bed as soon as her friends came in.

CHERYL *(angrily)*
What are you talking about?

FATHER
Now wait a minute—

KIM
And Brian wanted to give me some apple juice but she wouldn't let him cause it wouldn't be good for me—

CHERYL *(outraged)*
She's making that up!

KIM *(obliviously)*
But they were drinking apple juice and acting silly, but I didn't really want the apple juice, I just wanted the candy.

MOTHER
Candy?

CHERYL *(near tears)*
Mom! Make her stop!

KIM
They had all these little red candies, like vitamins, and they musta been good, only I couldn't have any—

MOTHER
I don't believe I'm hearing this—

CHERYL
Mom!

KIM
And they said it's vitamins so I wouldn't like'em, and I said "Well you sure like vitamins," and I had to go to my room.

FATHER
Now wait a minute—

MOTHER *(exasperated, to Father)*
Why don't you say something!

FATHER
Just . . . wait a minute!

Silence. He's on the spot, tries to talk rationally.

Now Cheryl, what about this? We go away for a weekend, we assume we can trust you. We asked you to take care of Kim, we asked you not to have any friends in the house, that wasn't too much to ask. Now I want the truth.

CHERYL
Whatta you want me to say?

FATHER
I want you to tell me the truth. Am I to understand that your friends came charging in here after midnight to drink apple juice and do vitamins?

CHERYL
Dad—

MOTHER
You're lying!

CHERYL
I haven't said a word!

FATHER
Now wait a minute—

CHERYL
I was here all evening, and Brian called me to go out but I said I couldn't, and I didn't, and there was nobody here except me and Kim, and she was a little monster, and she broke the vase in the den—

MOTHER *(automatically correcting)*
Vah-z—

CHERYL
And that's the truth.

FATHER
I want the truth.

CHERYL
That is the truth!

FATHER
Kim?

KIM
What?

FATHER
Are you telling the truth?

KIM
Well . . . actually . . . no.

FATHER
What really happened?

KIM
Well she didn't have a lotta friends drinking apple juice—

FATHER
That's better—

KIM
It was just Brian and they were drinking scotch.

Cheryl lets out a roar, attacks her. Kim escapes, off. Furious, Cheryl sits. Silence.

FATHER
Now Cheryl—

CHERYL
Is that what you think? Is that what you think of me?

MOTHER
Your father and I want the truth. Right now.

CHERYL
What I told you.

FATHER

Tell me the truth or you'll be grounded for a month—

CHERYL

If I tell you I didn't, you'll ground me, and if I tell you I did, you'll ground me, so you figure it out.

MOTHER

You don't talk to your father that way, young lady!

Silence. They look at one another, at a loss.

We thought we could trust you, go away for a weekend, have a little fun ourselves. We go out and we work every day for you to give you what you want—

KIM *(emerging, then retreating)*

Cheryl's in trouble!

CHERYL

Will you let me go kill her!

She starts up, then sits: a wad of tight rage.

I don't know what I'm sposed to say. If you don't believe me, then I might as well be doing whatever you think I'm doing. You always take her word for everything, but I'm telling the truth and I don't know what else to say.

MOTHER

That eye shadow looks terrible.

CHERYL

Mom!

FATHER

Now wait! Now we're going to get to the bottom of this. This is important. We're not going to let this drop. We're gonna crack down and we're gonna settle it.

That's all I've got to say.

Cheryl gets up, starts to go out.

MOTHER

Where are you going?

CHERYL

I'm going to my room.

MOTHER

You stay right here.

FATHER

Go to your room.

MOTHER
Do what your father tells you.

CHERYL
I am!

FATHER
Don't talk to your mother that way!

CHERYL
I'm not!

MOTHER
Don't yell at him!

FATHER
Just shape up!

MOTHER
And you're going to pay for that vase!

FATHER *(correcting automatically)*
Vah-z.

Cheryl rushes out in tears. Calling after her:

And you just stay up there till you decide you can act polite!

MOTHER *(calling after)*
Dinner's in ten minutes!

FATHER
We have to keep a firm hand.

MOTHER
It's a matter of being consistent.

They go out. Cheryl reappears upstage. Luann stands up, speaks to her.

LUANN
Cheryl?

CHERYL
Oh hi.

LUANN
How's it going? Hey. Get happy.

Cheryl turns away. Luann sits, head bowed. Cheryl moves to another area, with chairs arranged as a den, a stack of newspapers on the floor.

She picks up a paper, leafs through it, searching. Nick, her cousin, a few years older, enters with more newspapers.

NICK
Think this'll do?

CHERYL
I guess. Thanks for helping me with this.

NICK
What are cousins for?

CHERYL
Boy, how long's it been?

NICK
Three years, at Uncle Herbert's wedding.

CHERYL
Weddings, boy. . .

NICK
No, this is a great wedding. I'm getting rid of an older sister. What more can you ask?

CHERYL
Congratulations.

NICK *(indicating papers)*
So what am I looking for?

CHERYL
I don't believe she gave us an assignment like this. We have to find five articles on alcohol abuse.

NICK
Do ads count?

CHERYL
I guess.

NICK
How bout Uncle Herbert at the punch bowl? Can you hand him in?

They laugh.

CHERYL
Thanks for helping me with this. I always wait to the last minute, and it's due tomorrow, and I forgot we're coming to the wedding, so I walk in with a pile of newspapers to do my homework—

NICK
I used to do that all the time. My dad got so mad. Hey, here's one: "Three die in head-on crash." Cheerful stuff. *(looking at her)* I can't believe how much you've grown.

CHERYL
Just a little, I guess.

Tries to laugh. Then looks away.

NICK
What's the matter?

CHERYL
Nothing.

NICK
Hey. How long we known each other? What's wrong?

CHERYL
Well . . . I got a C in Algebra 2.

NICK
Is that all?

CHERYL
Oh. You know, same old stuff. Get up. Go to school. Come home. I'm really getting sick of it.

NICK
How bout your mom and dad?

CHERYL
They're fine. We can't stand each other.

NICK
Can't you talk to'em?

CHERYL
They don't trust me.

NICK
Should they?

CHERYL
I guess not. *(leafing impatiently)* I can't find anything in here. How'm I sposed to do this?

NICK
Here's one. "Alcohol factor in divorce."

CHERYL
This isn't helping anything! Hey Nick. . .

NICK
Huh?

CHERYL
Could I ask you a question?

NICK
Course.

CHERYL

You remember how your stepfather was drinking before? Was that hard to live with? I mean—

NICK

You better believe it.

CHERYL

I mean, if your mom didn't love him so much, would you want to go through that again?

NICK

What's wrong?

CHERYL

Was it really tough?

NICK

Yeh, it was. A lot of times it was really tough.

CHERYL

Are all men alike?

NICK

No. *(laughing)* Just similar.

CHERYL

I got a kind of a problem, kinda sorta, in a roundabout way, maybe. . .

NICK

Yeh?

CHERYL

Well, I've got a real close friend, and her name's, uh, Megan, and she's got this kinda problem with her boyfriend. . . And I wondered if you had any advice.

NICK

Well what's the problem?

CHERYL

Oh. Well this friend of mine, Megan, she's going with this guy, and she really likes him, I mean she'd marry him in a second, and he's really wonderful, he's smart and he's funny, and he bought her some earrings and. . .

She stops. He waits.

NICK

So the problem is what, that he drinks?

CHERYL

Well his whole family does. His dad's unemployed, and his

brother got kicked out of school, and then his brother was drinking and got in an accident, and there went his brother. But Brian doesn't drink that much— I mean this guy, my friend's boyfriend, he— doesn't drink that much. Just once in a while. It's not a real problem.

NICK

So it's not a real problem.

CHERYL

Well like, him and . . . my friend were at a party, and he was drinking, and she wasn't but he was, and he sorta got sick, and she stayed real late with him, and the next day she had a test and so she sort of failed it and brought down her grade, cause he was sort of drinking. . .

Pause.

It's so nice when he's ok. Cause boy, she gets so much flak from everybody, but he's so nice. You know how people say things that really hurt? They sting like nettles.

Pause.

This assignment just doesn't help anything!

Abruptly, she rips paper. Nick watches her. In the distance, others speak, sometimes singly, sometimes in unison, as if in Cheryl's memory.

VOICES

After all we've done for you.
You think you're so great.
She's really a character.
She's nothing special.
She's spoiled.
Grow up.
Be realistic.
Why aren't you more like your sister?
Did you actually write this? It seems too good.
Did you mean to do that with your eye shadow?
I used to like her a lot.
I used to trust her.
I used to think she was a lot of fun.
I used to think she was really special.
I used to be proud of her.

Cheryl looks through the newspapers, then stops.

NICK

Well look, why doesn't your friend try to help him? My stepdad, my mom told him he had to stop, but she loved him, and she'd help him, and they went to a clinic, she got him to a clinic and helped him stop.

CHERYL

Well this guy, I mean— What if he wouldn't? Cause he's got a lot to put up with, he deserves some happiness, doesn't he?

NICK

Does it make him happy?

CHERYL

Well I guess. He gets kinda loud and silly and funny and . . . kinda crazy . . . and then he gets mean. . .

But *she's* changed a lot. She's really messing up. She's losing her friends. She doesn't know what to do.

NICK

You probably drink some now and then yourself, don't you?

CHERYL

Well sure. No, not really. I mean only when I feel like it. Maybe to be sociable. I don't like the taste.

NICK

Well, what I would advise your friend is maybe talk to a counselor or—

CHERYL

I can't talk to a counselor! It's illegal for him to drink. I can't go in and say, "Excuse me, Brian's under age but he gets drunk every weekend and he sideswiped a car." He'll get in trouble!

NICK

Seems like trouble now.

CHERYL

Just forget the counselor, ok? Maybe he'll just quit. He said he was gonna quit.

NICK

You think he will?

CHERYL

No.

She looks at a newspaper.

Here's my horoscope. "Saturday, confide in someone you trust."

NICK
Cheryl, would you just level with me and tell me what you're—

VOICE *(off)*
Dinnertime!

CHERYL
That's ok. It's no big deal.

NICK
Look, this is important. Let's talk after dinner.

Cheryl gets up, stacks the papers.

CHERYL
No, we're taking off right after. Hey, it's no big deal. It's ok.

NICK
Really?

CHERYL
Yeh.

NICK
We'll talk another time.

CHERYL
Sure.

NICK
Well, we got three or four stories for you anyway. I'm gonna hit that punchbowl. Before Uncle Herbert drains it dry. I need it.

CHERYL
Me too.

They go. Luann stands up. Distant figures shift.

VOICES
She's nothing special.
She's spoiled.
Grow up.
Be realistic.
I used to like her a lot.
I used to trust her.
I used to think she was a lot of fun.
I used to think she was really special.
I used to be proud of her.

Cheryl reappears. Luann speaks to her.

LUANN
Cheryl?

No response.

Cheryl, we oughta talk. I mean it was an accident. And you know I knew there was some kinda problem—

CHERYL
Whatta you want?

LUANN
Talk to you.

CHERYL
So talk.

LUANN
You remember?

Cheryl moves to another area, chairs set as seats in an automobile. Luann walks into the area, with two others. They sit. Cheryl and Brian in front seat, Brian driving, Luann and Ken in back. Brian and Ken are loud and boisterous, Cheryl reserved.

What a bummer.

KEN
Hey, I liked it. It was a great movie. When she turns into a cockroach?

LUANN
Yuck.

CHERYL
I liked Elm Street One.

BRIAN *(making knife-finger gestures)*
Yahhh!

KEN
This one was second best. Two was the best, One was ok, Three was a ripoff—

BRIAN
You are brain-dead. Three was by far the best, except for One. Two was a total ripoff. This one was juvenile.

KEN
What about when the bones reassemble?

BRIAN
Why does she turn into a bug?

KEN
Cause she's afraid of bugs.

BRIAN
But where's it set up she's afraid of *being* a bug?

LUANN
Hey, guys—

KEN
I mean the whole point was when the camera goes down Freddy Kruger's mouth—

LUANN
It never does that.

BRIAN
It doesn't go down—

KEN
It goes down Freddy Kruger's mouth, and the point is, we're inside him—

LUANN *(disgusted)*
Oh yuck.

KEN
We're inside him, and that's why we can't escape him, cause we're really in his dream. That's the symbol of the movie.

LUANN
The symbol!

BRIAN
Lemme know when you've landed, Kenny. *(to Cheryl)* Whatta you think?

CHERYL
It was ok.

BRIAN
Whatta we do now?

LUANN
I'm hungry.

KEN
Let's hit the Burger King!

CHERYL
Hey, guys, I'm sorry, but I've gotta be home at eleven.

BRIAN
What?

CHERYL
I told you that. My dad's real mad, and he almost didn't let me go, and—

BRIAN
We got time.

KEN
Let's go to the Burger King.

LUANN
Hey no, if Cheryl has to get home, then take her home.

Brian yells out his window at another driver.

BRIAN
Hey jerkhead! Move it! Dumb trucker. Whose house can we go to?

CHERYL
Not mine.

KEN
Not mine.

BRIAN
Sure the hell not mine. Let's drive the loop.

LUANN
Cheryl's gotta get home.

BRIAN
Mind your own business.

CHERYL
Well I do.

BRIAN
I'm driving there, ok? Cheryl doesn't need you as spokesman.

CHERYL
Well Lu knows how much trouble I got in last time—

BRIAN
You know it doesn't make me feel so good that your parents think I'm some kinda monster, you gotta be in by eleven—

CHERYL
Brian—

LUANN *(to Brian)*
Will you lay off!

BRIAN
Lu, you are a real pain—

LUANN
You are a real pain also.

BRIAN
Why don't you get in the trunk? She can speak for herself, ok? *(to Cheryl)* What about it, you wanna go home?

CHERYL
Yes I do.

BRIAN
What, I guess you agree with your parents, huh? I'm a real loser, my family's all bums, huh?

LUANN
Just take her home!

BRIAN
I am!

KEN *(trying to add cheer)*
What I don't understand is why the soccer team doesn't get cheerleaders. Football players get cheerleaders, and we had a better season than the football team. Everybody had a better season than the football team. The cheerleaders had a better season. The roaches in the cafeteria had a lot better season.

No response.

I think we're fading fast.

CHERYL *(indicating)*
That's my turn.

LUANN
Slow down.

CHERYL
Brian—

LUANN
You passed the turn.

BRIAN
We'll go back.

LUANN
Then go back.

BRIAN
Wait for an exit.

LUANN
You did that deliberately.

KEN
Hey guys—

LUANN
Brian, you got her in trouble before, she's gotta be home by eleven—

BRIAN
Choke her for me, Kenny—

CHERYL
Brian, what's the matter? You never act like this if you haven't been—

BRIAN *(mimicking)*
If I haven't been what?

CHERYL
Drinking.

KEN *(referring to movie)*
Hey, how bout when the chick is on the beach—

BRIAN *(calling out window)*
Hey grandpa, it's past your bedtime! Whatta these old guys doing out so late?

LUANN
You are the most totally selfish person I know.

BRIAN
Kill her, Kenny.

LUANN
Touch me and die, Kenny.

BRIAN
Don't worry, hon, no guy would ever touch you.

LUANN
You want children later in life, Brian?

BRIAN
Not from you.

KEN
Guys, hey, cool it. Guess what? Party time!

Ken brings out pint of bourbon.

Let's get happy.

BRIAN
All right!

LUANN
Where'd you get that?

KEN
The tooth fairy.

CHERYL *(timidly)*
Brian, you're driving.

LUANN *(adamantly)*
Come on, put it away. Kenny, now put that away.

KEN
Hey. Don't worry. Get happy!

CHERYL *(urgently)*
Brian, please—

BRIAN
I'm driving you home, ok? After we go round the loop a little.

LUANN
Let me drive. I'm not gonna ride with somebody that's drinking.

BRIAN
Then get out.

CHERYL
Brian, were you drinking at the movie?

BRIAN
So what?

CHERYL
You told me you wouldn't—

BRIAN
Yes Mommy.

KEN
Hey guys— Hey, sport, at least one hand on the wheel, please?

LUANN
Look, macho man, Cheryl has to be home at eleven cause you got drunk—

BRIAN
Yes Mommy.

LUANN
And it's illegal to drink when you're driving—

BRIAN
"And you're underage—"

LUANN
And you're underage—

BRIAN
Yes Mommy!

KEN
Hey—

CHERYL
Lu, please—

LUANN
And your brother and your old man were drunks and you're on the way!

CHERYL *(enraged)*
Lu, you don't know anything about that, just mind your own business, I can take care of myself—

LUANN *(simultaneously)*
Don't yell at me, I'm trying to help, you're letting this jerk walk all over you and I'm not going to let you mess up your life—

BRIAN *(exploding)*
Just shut up!

KEN
Hey. We're having fun.

Silence.

LUANN
This is the last time we do this.

CHERYL
Brian, I just wish we could. . . You've got me home late every night, and I like you a lot, but—

BRIAN
She likes me a lot, hear that?

CHERYL *(gathering courage)*
But I don't like you when you drink. I really don't like it. I wish you'd stop.

BRIAN
Let's have fun.

Turns on car radio loud. Accelerates.

LUANN
Slow down.

BRIAN
No, Cheryl's gotta get home. I gotta get her home.

CHERYL
Brian, don't go so fast.

KEN
Brian—

BRIAN
No, she's gonna be late, she's gonna be in big trouble, we gotta get her home, faaaaaast!

They begin to panic. Ad lib.

KEN
Hey come on, sport—

CHERYL
Brian, please—

BRIAN
"Please?" Sure, anything to please.

LUANN
Slow down!

BRIAN
Yes Mommy!

KEN
Brian, slow down—

BRIAN
Yes Mommy!

CHERYL
Look out!

All look forward. Actors freeze. Others move off slowly, leaving Cheryl. Luann sits in her chair far right. Others group upstage, watching Cheryl.

LUANN
I don't see her much now. She was my best friend, and you just don't think. . .
It coulda been worse. It coulda been a lot worse. None of us got really hurt, except Cheryl, and she's back in school, she missed a lot, but she's catching up, I mean she was really lucky, they thought she was gonna be paralyzed, but she's just got kind of a limp. . .
But she doesn't talk to me. She doesn't talk to anybody.
Once I asked her, "What would you really like somebody to say to you? In your wildest dreams?"

As individual voices are heard, Cheryl rises, walks, with a slight limp, into center.

VOICES
I love you, Cheryl.
I'm proud you're my daughter.
You're doing awesome in Algebra 2.
I like your hair.
I'm glad to be your friend.

LUANN

She was always a lot of fun, we'd start laughing—

I knew her ever since we were little. We'd get on some real serious topic, feeling sorry for ourselves, and then one of us'd say something dumb, and start laughing and—

Once we put on this reeky perfume and ran through the mall, and all these little old ladies yelling at us, and then find out we're both allergic, and we both swole up like balloons.

Laughs, then suddenly angry:

She was so dumb. She'd make really stupid jokes, and they were never that funny. She liked to fib. She'd let people walk all over her, and then she'd do something stupid.

VOICES

We love you.

We want to help you.

Talk to me.

LUANN

But we'd start laughing, we couldn't stop. Middle of a restaurant, it was embarrassing, we fell out of our chairs, laughing.

Pause.

And Brian wasn't hurt. He's in big trouble, but he wasn't hurt.

But I mean she was my friend. I'm talking like she was dead. I don't mean that.

But there was a family in the other car. And they had a little boy, five-year-old, and. . .

VOICES *(in unison)*

We love you.

LUANN

It wasn't Cheryl's fault.

VOICES

We want to help you.

LUANN

Nobody blames her.

VOICES

You're my friend.

LUANN

I wish she'd talk to me.

VOICES

Talk to me.

LUANN
We were always laughing.

VOICES
Talk to me.

Cheryl remains motionless, staring at us. Lights fade.

Success

Characters

Nick. 20. Unemployed.
Leslie. 21. Store clerk. Single mother.
Sam. 21. Pre-med student.
Reality. An older person, in hat and sunglasses.

Setting

An open stage, with chairs, table, and bench. At the outset, these are set to represent a restaurant booth. Later, the actors reset them to represent Leslie's living room, then a playground. Another chair at the far right.

If a scenic backdrop is desired, we suggest a flat, painted backdrop with a collage of elements: senior class photos, want ads, or other images derived from the text.

Notes

This play was created through scripting based on two weeks of intensive improvisations by a group of Philadelphia actors in our developmental Genesis Ensemble. It was then toured to approximately twenty-five high schools in the Greater Philadelphia region, with many rewrites during that tour.

We were interested in that odd span of time after high school when people go "out into the world" — most to college, it's expected, where they do indeed face new realities, but delay, for a time, facing Reality. It's a time when old ties dissolve, new ones form, and when, for many, decisions are made faster than they like. For a cast of high school students, we recommend that part of rehearsal exploration on this play should be to talk with people who are in that time span, or older people who can remember their years immediately following high school.

This play is probably more difficult than others in the volume to perform for large audiences. There's a plot and a progression, yes, but also longer scenes of soul-searching discussion. The key to keeping it lively, we've found, is to remember that these three characters are all in a highly *volatile* state. Coming back together is a difficult challenge: they feel judged, and they're judging themselves. As young as they are, they feel trapped in a dead-end or treadmill condition. They want to be together, yet they don't. Everyone is highly keyed to react, so there's much more explosive potential — sudden bursts of laughter, sudden flares of temper, sudden silences — than if they were just a casual group of friends getting together for coffee. This gives the play a vitality that's absolutely essential, especially in the first scene, to sustain interest.

The character of Reality can be male or female, any age. If cast with an actress, a few lines will need to be changed. The sole requirement is that he or she can relate well with the audience through a mask of mock hostility, and be always in total control — because it's Reality. Reality isn't malevolent; he just requires honesty, which can be challenging at times. When entering into the roles of waiter, boss, and friend in different scenes, the performer should play them realistically. Our Reality wore a fedora and mirror sunglasses — with the unsettling sense that he'll never quite let us see his intention.

Scene shifts should be as simple and rapid as possible, so we suggest that the same furniture be used — a row of chairs rather than a sofa, for example. If realistic furniture were used for Leslie's living room, then we'd expect full-scale playground equipment for the next scene.

On the other hand, the props and costumes should be completely real and should be chosen with great care. Since Nick is traveling, does he have a shoulder bag with him? What's in it? Exactly how much money does he have in his pockets? What's all the litter that Leslie's trying to pick up? What does Sam have along that he needs to study? What do people have in their pockets? Creating these small realities at the outset of rehearsal is a challenge for character analysis, and will perhaps yield interesting scenic detail; but above all, it makes the characters real to the actors themselves.

Despite the presence of an abstract character, direct address to the audience, etc., the play is realistic. That is, what's essential to the audience is a sense that they're seeing accurately observed, true behavior. Everything is in the service of that.

SUCCESS

Leslie and Sam appear. Leslie speaks to us.

LESLIE
You know how you're going along, one day after another, and then suddenly Bam! You get hit by a truck.
Or like if you meet— *(to one of us)* What's your name? *(a response, e.g. "Brian.")* Like if you meet Brian!
In high school, we were all on the Yearbook Committee—

SAM *(interrupting)*
I had *no* interest in the yearbook — the *yearbook*?— but I was planning on college, so Mr. Haverstick said, "You need extracurricular activities."
So we were on this committee— Me and Leslie and this other girl, Sandy, and Nick, this really smart guy— He was always in your face, but you knew, you just knew he was gonna make it. He was awesome.

LESLIE
And then one day— One day Nick brought in these cartoons he did, and "maybe we use these in the yearbook." Cartoons of everybody, the teachers, the basketball team, the lunchroom— and they were *funny*. They were *life*.
But the one that got us in trouble—

Reality, from the audience, honks a goose horn. Leslie looks at him.

REALITY
She talks too much.

Nick appears, speaks to us:

NICK
I was scared. I never showed my stuff to nobody, showed to my mom once, she said, "That's cute." But they liked it. That felt so good.
The one I did for the cover, it was a circus, and the teachers were clowns, and the principal, he was the bearded lady, and that kinda caused some trouble—

Reality honks. Nick looks at him. Reality speaks to us, as others set for the next scene.

REALITY
I like doing this. Let me ask you something: show of hands, ok? How many think you're ever gonna get out of high school? Like you'll spend the rest of your life right here?

Gestures for a show of hands.

How many of you, right now, can think of some place you'd rather be?

Hands.

Well too-o-o bad. But that's Reality, right?

NICK
Who are you?

REALITY
Reality. Don't you know me when you see me? Also known as Grim Reality, Harsh Reality, Empirical Reality, Naked Reality, woo! Stark Reality, The Nitty Gritty, The Way Of The World, or As Sure As God Made Little Green Apples. Reality.

NICK
Get outa my face.

REALITY
You're cute when you're mad.

Nick leaves. Sam sits at a cafe table, writing in his notebook. Leslie appears, followed by Nick. They sneak up behind him, grab him:

LESLIE & NICK
Sam!!!

He reacts. All laugh, greet, ad lib.

SAM
You're both on time. Amazing.

NICK
We ran into each other outside.

SAM
Where'd you go after the reception?

NICK
I walked around. Went out to the playground.

LESLIE
Playground?

NICK
Where we hung out and planned the yearbook.

SAM
Always the drifter.

Reality, as a waiter, tosses menus on table, goes.

This is freaky, I haven't seen you guys, what, three years? Summer after graduation?

LESLIE
We're out of high school! Yes!

SAM
You haven't changed.

LESLIE
Oh no? I'm a mommy now.

SAM
Oh right—

LESLIE
Tonya's two and a half.

SAM
She got all her shots?

NICK
Hey, Doctor Sam!

SAM
Don't call me that. I'm just finishing pre-med.

NICK
Doctor Sam!

Reality returns.

REALITY
Something to eat?

LESLIE
Decaf.

NICK
Cup of coffee, and you got a doughnut?

SAM
Tea. Hey, does Martha still work here?

REALITY
Who?

SAM
Martha was a waitress here?

No response. Reality goes. They grimace at his unfriendliness.

LESLIE
It's so strange to see you guys. Sandy said she was going to invite everybody to the wedding, but I didn't know you'd come. How'd she find your address?

NICK
She sent it to my mother. I was in Seattle.

LESLIE
Seattle, wow.

NICK
Checking out possibilities.

SAM
The wedding was great.

NICK
May she have many more!

Leslie hits him playfully.

Sandy's guy is kinda goofy-looking.

LESLIE
He's cute!

NICK
Bright red hair?

SAM
It's amazing. You were the last people I would have hung with—

LESLIE
You either—

SAM
And Haverstick pushed us into it and said, "Make it something you'll remember four years from now." And we did.

LESLIE
We did.

SAM
You wrote some great stuff.

LESLIE
I forgot about that. I remember Nick's drawings. Hey, where's the cartoons? I know you're doing something!

NICK
You were the editor—

SAM
The Principal vetoes the cover, says, "Education is not a circus, and I am not a clown."

NICK

This story gets bigger as time goes on.

SAM

I stuck up for you, dummy!

NICK

How you organized that protest—

SAM

No sweat.

LESLIE

No sweat? You were gonna be suspended, you wouldn't get into college. No big deal?

Oh, the wedding was great, but I really wanted to talk to Sandy. I mean, she started college, and then she got into this thing to be an electrician. She really loves it. How did she do that?

NICK

Money.

SAM

For your information, Sandy's mom's a bookkeeper, her dad's on disability. Not everybody does it with money.

NICK

Med students got money.

SAM

Money? I got loans, I got scholarships, I work two jobs in the summer, I work at school—

NICK

So you're a workaholic.

SAM

When did you ever do a day's work? You're three times as smart as I am, I don't see you doing nothing with it.

NICK

I got plans.

SAM

Let me tell you something about Reality. Summers I'm working as a flunkey at a hospital, plus a night job—

NICK

Busy busy!

SAM

So the director calls me in—

In another area, Reality appears as a supervisor.

REALITY
Mr. Rusk. Correct me if I'm wrong, it appears you're coming in at 7:30 a.m.—

SAM *(moving into the area)*
Yes?

REALITY
Where the shift starts at seven a.m.

SAM
Ok. Before you came, the director gave me special permission to come at 7:15, cause the bus gets here either a half hour early or a couple minutes late. And I'm working a night job, I have to get up at 5:30, but I get everything done ok, so—

REALITY
Special permission. What line is that under? "Special permission?"

SAM
No, she did it as a favor.

REALITY
If we do favors for one employee, we'll have everyone coming at us.

SAM
Well ask'em. Linda, Mark, they're fine with it.

REALITY
I need you here at seven.

SAM
If you want me at seven, I need to be twenty minutes early, or fifteen minutes late.

REALITY
You want to come in early that's fine.

SAM
Would I get overtime?

REALITY
No.

SAM
I'll have to get up at five.

REALITY
That's your problem.

Reality raises the goose horn, honks directly at him. He goes back to the cafe. Nick rises.

NICK
What I'm telling you—

LESLIE
Guys, let's not fight. Sandy's off doing her thing, honeymoon, that stuff, and we haven't seen each other, so let's celebrate.

NICK
Great.

SAM
Movie? Something cheap.

LESLIE
Problem is, though, I've got Tonya, and the babysitter leaves in a half hour, and Dave was supposed to take her today, for the weekend, but he didn't show and—

SAM
Who's Dave?

LESLIE
Tonya's dad. My ex.

NICK
Good ole Dave.

LESLIE
So maybe, like, you could come over to my place, we could get a pizza, *(to Nick)* show us some new cartoons, and you could see Tonya—

NICK
Real hot time.

LESLIE
Or I could call Dave and scream at him and maybe he'd show up, and then we could go out.

NICK
Let's all call him. "Da-ave!"

LESLIE *(exasperated)*
I'll go call.

She gets up, goes out. Reality, as waiter, comes in with the check. Both calling after her:

SAM & NICK
"Da-ave!"

Laughter, then silence.

NICK
Hey, I'm sorry, man, I'm not doing real hot right now.

SAM
Yeh?

NICK
I thought I had something in Seattle, but it didn't work out. So I was wondering if you could help me out.

SAM
Cup of coffee, doughnut, be my guest.

NICK
I might have this thing in Chicago, friends starting this company to design web pages, I mean it's good money, I'd pay you back right away and—

SAM
Money? Nick, I don't have it.

NICK
You got a credit card? Put it on your credit card.

SAM
I'm working twenty hours a day—

NICK
Think about it.

Leslie returns.

LESLIE
Think about what?

SAM
Life.

LESLIE
He's coming. He said right away, that means an hour.

NICK
I forgot my wallet.

SAM
I'll pay.

NICK *(to Sam)*
Can I ride with you?

SAM
Sure. *(to Leslie)* You wanta leave the tip?

NICK
Leave'im a tip. Here's a tip. "Drop dead."

They start to go. Reality honks. They freeze.

REALITY
What's happening, Sam?

SAM

Like I really want to have fun and stop thinking about school, but I'm spending time with these people trying to grab onto something that doesn't exist any more.

REALITY

Nick?

NICK

They're judging me. "Are you really the genius we thought you were?" I gotta get some money.

REALITY

Leslie?

LESLIE

I want to show'em my home, and Tonya, and carpet and curtains— I want'em to like it. Cause that's all I got.

They reset the scene. Reality speaks to us.

REALITY

Questions. How many of you have an idea what you're gonna be doing in ten years?

Indicates show of hands.

How many are gonna definitely win the Lottery or play in the NBA?

Hands.

How many of you look at the future and really don't like what you see? Really mad sometimes? Yeh. Mad. Really mad. Really really mad!

Well sorry bout that.

He honks, disappears. Leslie's apartment, pillows scattered, child's toys on the floor. Leslie hurries to straighten things up. Knock at door. She rushes to open it. Nick and Sam enter.

LESLIE

I just got here. Make yourself comfortable. The babysitter, I gotta pay her. I'm gonna call Dave again.

SAM

Can we see Tonya?

LESLIE

I don't want to get her revved up. You can see her asleep.

Leslie goes out. Sam and Nick come into the room. Nick picks up a clown doll, toys with it.

NICK
Sam, look, I would never ask you for money—

SAM
My mistake. I thought I heard "Sam, I need a hundred fifty bucks—"

NICK
Well make it a hundred.

SAM
See, I thought we were here because we were friends—

NICK
That's why I'm asking you.

SAM
And you got these things going, and I don't have a life. I am maybe gonna have a life in ten years, if my girlfriend doesn't get tired of waiting, and you're asking me for money so—

NICK
Forget it—

SAM
So you can cat around to Seattle and—

NICK
Forget it!

SAM
I will!

NICK *(tossing the doll away)*
Clowns give me the creeps.

Leslie returns.

LESLIE
He's not there. Maybe he's left.

SAM
How long you been on your own?

LESLIE
Two and a half years. Tonya's two and a half. Dave couldn't quite deal with being a dad. So he split.

NICK
Nice apartment. You working?

LESLIE
No, the bank just likes me and gives me money. Yes I'm working. Clothing store.

NICK
So you the manager?

LESLIE
Retail clerk.

NICK
Well, onward and upward.

LESLIE
It's a dead-end job, ok? I can't afford to keep it and I can't afford to quit. Day care's killing me, I don't have health insurance, he's not paying child support—
I'll tell you something about Reality. There was an opening, Assistant Manager. And I went in to talk to the Manager. . .

Scene shifts. Reality appears.

Do you have a minute?

REALITY
Sure.

LESLIE
Well, Sharon said, a couple weeks ago she said she was leaving and there'd be an opening, and I was wondering—

REALITY
Yes, in fact I wanted to talk to you about that.

LESLIE
Oh. Ok.

REALITY
We've filled that position. She'll be starting next week.

LESLIE
Was it advertised?

REALITY
No, we go through an agency. I think you'll like working with her, but the thing is, she's just out of college, she doesn't have a lot of experience, so I'd appreciate it if you could help train her. You know the job as well as Sharon did.

LESLIE
So you want me to—

REALITY
And kind of fill in for her till she gets up to speed, ok?

LESLIE
I was just curious what kind of requirements there are for a job like that.

REALITY
Well, college degree, that stuff. Anything else?

LESLIE
No.

Back to the scene.

NICK
I'd quit. I wouldn't stay there five minutes.

SAM
Yeh! Let's take an example from Nick! He don't take nothin' from nobody! Where's your phone? I'm gonna call some clubs, see who's playing.

LESLIE
Kitchen.

He goes out. Nick picks up a doll, uses it as puppet.

NICK
"I'm sorry, Leslie."

LESLIE *(going along with the game)*
That's ok.

NICK
"I'm sad."

LESLIE
Don't be sad.

NICK
"Cause I'm broke. And Raggedy Ann won't give me any raggedy money. Cause I need to get to Chicago, and so I need a hundred bucks."

LESLIE *(playing)*
Ok. Here's a hundred bucks.

NICK *(directly to her)*
I mean really. I could pay you off in a month, there's a job in a restaurant—

LESLIE
Nick, are you serious? I'm having trouble even paying the rent.

NICK
I know. I hate to ask you, but—

SAM *(off)*
Somebody's at the door.

LESLIE
Hold on.

She goes out, as Sam returns. Voices off.

NICK *(with the doll)*
"Hi, Sammy! Are we still friends?"

SAM
Did you ask her for money?

NICK
I would never ask her for money.

SAM
Ok, I called about bus tickets. It's a hundred forty bucks to Chicago. I'll stop at a Mac machine. Just pay me back next month—

NICK
Oh Sam, thanks, man—

SAM
And don't slobber on me. Just take it.

Quarrel offstage. Leslie at last screams, "Get lost!" She enters.

LESLIE *(brightly)*
Let's go out.

They start to go. Reality honks.

REALITY
What's happening, Sam?

SAM
It's a hustle, I know it is, but I can't say no.

REALITY
Leslie?

LESLIE
A hundred bucks. I can't afford *ten* bucks. How could he ask me for that? I'll stop at a Mac machine.

REALITY
Nick?

NICK
I got the money, and I feel like slime.

They reset scene. Reality speaks, asks for hands.

REALITY
How many of you would loan your friend money?
How many of you feel really responsible to somebody, that you need to fulfill a responsibility to somebody else?

How many of you think *I* am your friend?
Well, you'd be surprised.

New setting: the park. Chairs and a stepladder define play equipment, benches. They scatter, in high spirits, exploring.

LESLIE
It's our playground! It's exactly the same!

SAM
Even the graffiti.

NICK
They changed the swings. Plastic seats.

SAM
They always had plastic seats. You're out of touch with what you're sitting on.

LESLIE
I loved this place. Watching you guys act like little kids, and Sandy was queen of the monkey bars.

SAM
I need more playground. If I could— Ok, like set a goal and work as hard as it takes. But then, play on the playground. Spend all day saving my patients with my fantastic skills, and then we play on the playground. That's success.
What about you?

LESLIE
Success? Forget it. Ok. Raise my kid. That's it. Make her happy. Try to make me happy. I'd like to have some friends.

SAM
What about you?

NICK
This is freaky. Let's go.

SAM
You said you wanted to stop here.

LESLIE
Nick, when we gonna see some cartoons?

NICK
I dunno.

LESLIE
I mean it! I want to see what you been doing!

NICK
Wasn't there a statue there?

SAM
You were the statue there.

NICK
What?

SAM
You were. Summer after graduation, and you got fired or something, and we were looking for you all over, came here, you were standing up on the rock there like *(imitating)*, "Don't come close! I'm gonna jump!"

NICK
I remember that. Yeh, you were talking about Reality? Ok. I met him. I met him that summer.

Nick approaches Reality, sitting on a bench.

Hey Jack!

REALITY
What's happening?

NICK
Well I was gonna ask you. Hey, I got some new drawings—

REALITY
I love your stuff.

NICK
It got me fired.

REALITY
Huh?

NICK
Crazy. I was on my break, and the foreman came up, "What's that?" "Well, it's kind of a cartoon, about my view of society, and—" "That looks like me." "Well it's a foreman." Then he says, "I am not amused by this," and he fired me.

REALITY
That's heavy.

NICK
So I wondered if you'd had a chance to show it to your editor.

REALITY
Yeh, no, I mean, well, yeh. . .

NICK
And then I go home, and my mom gets at me, "Why you doing

that comic stuff?" And I say, "Mom, this is me." She says, "This is cartoons! Are you Mickey Mouse?" It's crazy. I told her you might publish it and I make some money, she says, "What guarantee?" "What's for dinner, Mom?" "Jus' draw yourself a cartoon of a turkey, an' eat that!"

REALITY
Yeh, well your stuff is really cool. But it might not be the right time for it, you know?

NICK
Whatta you mean, you said it was—

REALITY
You gotta fit the whole kinda . . . ambience.

NICK
Did the editor see it?

REALITY
Yeh.

NICK
What did he say?

REALITY
Nick—

NICK
What did he say? I want to know what he said.

REALITY
He said, I quote, "They're too cartoony."

NICK
"Too cartoony?"

REALITY
"And the guy can't draw."

Scene dissolves. Nick broods.

LESLIE
Nick, that's crazy. That's one guy. That was three years ago. Come on.

NICK
Yes, Mr. Haverstick.

LESLIE
Nick—

SAM
Nick. I'm sorry I got kinda mad. I hope this helps out. Pay me back when you can.

Gives him money. Leslie sees it.

LESLIE
Ok. So I guess you won't be needing this.

Shows bills. Sam realizes.

SAM *(enraged)*
Did you ask her for money? Did you?

NICK
Just give me some space.

LESLIE
Nick—

SAM
A single mother, working like hell, and she doesn't have— *(grabbing bills)* Gimme my money!

LESLIE
Let me talk! Nick, I'm gonna do you a great favor.

NICK
Forget the money.

LESLIE
I'm not gonna forget the money. I'm gonna rub your nose in it. In a week I could be out on the street, with a child, and you could care less—

NICK
So all right!

LESLIE
I'm gonna give you the opportunity, the once in a lifetime opportunity, to grow up. You're gonna take some responsibility—

NICK
Ok!

LESLIE
You get down on your knees and say "Thank you Leslie! Thank you Leslie, for telling me to grow the hell up and be a man!"

She turns away. Long silence.

SAM
It's getting pretty late, I think it's time to—

Nick rises and confronts them, vehemently.

NICK
Don't you think I try? You know what it's like to wake up every morning and say what am I doing here? You think this is fun?

"You can do it, Nick! Do anything you want!" What am I supposed to want? How do I know what I'm supposed to want?!

Silence.

Success? For me, that's if there's one human being on the face of the earth who really gives a damn whether I live or die. That's it. That's it. Simple, huh?

LESLIE *(after a moment, quietly)*
Nick, it's ok for you to run around and feel sorry for yourself, but in the meantime tend to business.

SAM
Right.

LESLIE
And you, Sammy, tend to business, but in the meantime, stop feeling so sorry for yourself. Act human.

SAM
Want to play tennis?

No response.

Remember we played air tennis here? *(to Nick)* Your serve.

NICK
No thanks.

Sam tosses him an imaginary ball. No response. Another toss. Nick tosses it back. Sam hits it. Sam and Leslie begin a volley. Then they stop, stand waiting for Nick. At last he gets up, begins playing.

Reality appears. As he honks, they freeze, each character responds, then the game continues.

REALITY
Tomorrow, Sam, it's back to the grind.

SAM
Yeh. But I have to learn how to have a life. I have to work, but I've gotta have a life.

Game continues. He honks. Freeze.

REALITY
You're trapped, Leslie. Twenty-two years old, you're trapped.

LESLIE
Maybe I am, maybe I'm not. Maybe I find the money, go back to school, make a future.

Game continues. He honks. Freeze.

REALITY

So, you still thinking about suicide, Nick?

NICK

No, not right now. We're together now, so it's ok. I'm not as lonely now.

They continue playing. A strong rally, fantastic volleys, and at last Nick scores. Sam hugs him.

LESLIE

Nick.

They look at her.

Let's do something for real. Not a game. You did something for me. You take this money, and use it for whatever, and pay me back every nickel or may you rot in hell.

Holds out money.

SAM

You asked for it. You got it. Deal with it.

Holds out money.

NICK

I don't want to owe you.

LESLIE

Take it, Nick. You owe us. You owe us.

SAM

Are we gonna stay in touch?

Nick hesitates, then takes the money. Freeze. As Reality speaks, they break to new positions.

REALITY

What happens now? What happens to these people in a year? Or five years? What do you think happens to Leslie? If you could make up the story, whatta you think?

Ad lib to draw audience response.

What about Sam? Is he gonna stick with it?

Responses.

What about Nick? Does he pay back the money? Who says no? What do you think happens? Where is he in five years?

Responses.

Does anybody think he will pay it back, and do something with his life? What happens to him? Make up his story.

Responses.

We don't know how the story goes. Here's one way it could go. A year later.

The trio stand at a distance, talking by phone, two at a time. Sam and Leslie:

SAM

I heard from Sandy. She's expecting. Twins.

LESLIE

I hope it's not contagious.

They shift. Leslie and Nick:

Did Sam call you?

NICK

Not for a while.

LESLIE

I talked to him, he finished his first semester med school. Just barely. Said he's decided he needs a hobby, so. . .

NICK

He's getting married?

She nods. They shift. Nick and Sam:

I called her, and she's taking classes at the community college, plus working full time, and she sounded half dead, but happy.

Sam and Leslie:

SAM

He paid me back. Did he pay you back?

LESLIE

Last month.

SAM

Unbelievable.

REALITY

It might go that way. It might go a dozen ways. Make your own story. That's what Nick and Sam and Leslie are doing. Making their own story.

NICK

This is not necessarily a happy ending.

LESLIE

I'll settle for happy beginnings.

They come forward, link hands. Fade.

Dividing Lines

NOTES

The genesis of *Dividing Lines* was a commission from Franklin & Marshall College to produce a show as the keynote to a campus-wide "Day of Diversity." We were challenged to introduce a wide range of issues in a polarized atmosphere: many students and faculty anticipated merely a time-wasting liberal guilt-trip. So it had to be funny, it had to be forty minutes, and it had to work at ten a.m. in the college gym.

In fact, it was successful and led to a series of new shows, under the same title, commissioned by Germantown Academy, Agnes Irwin School, and University of the Arts, developed through improvisations with student casts. In 1995, we reworked the best pieces with a professional cast and produced it at Old City Stage Works in Philadelphia.

While some pieces were created solely with one group, others were carried on to other casts and further adapted. Two sketches were engendered during a college residency fifteen years earlier, and *Ceremonies in Concrete* and *Evaluation* go back to our first ensemble, Theatre X, nearly thirty years ago. Deriving a scenario from an existing piece, then improvising and scripting a new piece from that scenario can be fruitful, and we offer groups the freedom to try it with this material.

The twelve dramatic micro-plays included here are from four different productions of *Dividing Lines*. They're intended to be selected and combined according to the talents and interests of the producing group.

PRODUCING THE SHOW

The micro-plays have casts of from two to nine performers; with doubling, everything can be performed with six. Or it's possible to do a show using different people in each sketch. Our own practice is to use a relatively small cast, so that the audience has the pleasure of seeing one person play a variety of roles.

We suggest that furnishings be as simple as possible, simply changing arrangements of table and chairs between pieces.

The micro-plays range from approximately two to fifteen minutes in length. Before finalizing selections for a show, you should rehearse and time each piece. We've performed them in combinations ranging from thirty minutes to two hours.

Finding the order of the pieces — "routining" the show — isn't easy. There are many contrasts to balance: light vs. heavy, comic vs. serious, small-cast vs. full ensemble, active vs. static, artificial vs. realistic, stand-up vs. sit-down. Sometimes one piece leads logically to another; sometimes you want the most radical contrast. Experiment.

For "openers," we tend to use larger-cast, more theatrical pieces, less based in a realistic story. *Musical Chairs* and *Ceremonies in Concrete* have worked well as openers. The essential thing is to establish the energy of the show. If you open on a quieter tone, then your second piece should be high-energy.

For us, the closing piece usually brings a larger number of people onto stage and obviously must have a feeling of finality. Of these pieces, *Dinner Party* and *Party Time* have been effective as closers. But again, experiment.

A few specific notes. Short sketches require a special precision in acting. The whole story and the characters are established in a few lines. Changes in tone may happen very quickly. There's no waste space. They require a lot of very specific work in tempo and timing, very concrete choices in physical action.

Dinner Party presents special problems. The long litanies of foreign foods require, first, that someone spend a long time at the library looking up pronunciations, and a great deal of group drill. In our production, music was composed for the final sequence, and the actors went into a choreographed round dance. It really requires a musical-comedy sensibility, especially at the climax.

These pieces aren't preachments about issues; they're depictions of human behavior. For example, *All-Nighter* shows the consequences of someone telling a demeaning joke, but the piece works only if each actor plays his or her character as being completely in the right, completely justified. Let us, the audience, make our own judgments.

Musical Chairs

Lights. Characters wander in, as if at a meeting, circulating, ad lib conversation. One man sets chairs in a circle. After a moment:

KEVIN

Ok? Could I have your attention? Let's take our seats and get started.

All sit, except one. He looks around for a chair.

TIM

Hey, guys, I don't like to express the obvious, but doesn't this look just a little tacky here? I mean, First One Out?

SONJA

Listen, we know what you're thinking. But look, the rules are the same for everybody. Everybody's got the same chance.

TIM

But not everybody's got a chair.

KEVIN

You have a chance for a chair. That's even better. If everybody had a chair—

CHRIS

If we all had a chair, we wouldn't see the value of chairs.

J.J.

We'd lose that competitive edge.

TIM

Look. I am educated, I am polite, I have something to contribute to this meeting, this is a country founded on the ideals of tolerance and mutual respect, and still I am left standing.

SONJA

Well that's part of your cultural heritage.

TIM

Ok. So be it. I don't understand, really. But I'm cool. There's not room for everybody, and somebody has to gracefully bow out, and I'll gracefully bow out. No problem. Just next time maybe you could tell me who's invited and who's not and give me a little warning you're going to do this and I'LL BE ABLE TO HANDLE IT!!!

Music. All rise, circulate. The loser takes chair, turns it over, goes to the edge, stands watching. Music stops. All scramble and sit. J.J. is left out.

J.J.

It's a game. A silly damn game. This is a kid's game and you just never grow up. And this game is rigged. It's a test of aggressiveness, pushiness, conniving. Are those the genetic traits we want to encourage? I mean you just blow my mind! It's not just a game, dammit. There are consequences. There are some who are In and some left Out, and I'm Out. How do you justify this to yourselves? It doesn't help to say, "Well the rules are the same. The ban on sleeping in doorways applies to rich and poor alike." Being In or Out has consequences!

CHRIS

Hey, but you've come a long way!

SONJA

You're poised on the verge.

JOY

Don't think negative, J.J. Is a glass half empty or half full? Don't think of you standing up. Think of us sitting down.

KEVIN

What are you so upset for? So you don't have a chair. So sit on my lap.

Music. J.J. turns over a chair, goes to the side, stands. All circulate. Music stops. All scramble and sit. Chris is left out.

CHRIS

Oh. Well. Yes. I was expecting this. It's perfectly in keeping with the devaluation of what's referred to, how do they say it, the *dominant paradigm*? Now I've been teaching Herman Melville for nineteen years, my Melville notes are part of our cultural heritage— but I know. They say no one cares about Herman Melville any more. It's not relevant. It's not Politically Correct to kill large mammals. We have to make room for the full range of world cultures, and if something New comes in then something Old goes out. Knowledge expands, but the curriculum is finite, four courses a semester, so, well then, some century has to go, it either has to be the 20th or the 19th, because the 16th has the Dean behind it. But there is a purpose in teaching Herman Melville!—

JOY

To reinforce the patriarchal culture. Ahab is raping the whale. He is exploiting the entire Third World—

CHRIS

The whale is a White Whale. A White Whale! Not a Multicultural Whale!

KEVIN

Whales will be obsolete in the 21st Century. We can put an entire whale on a microchip.

CHRIS

Ahab and the Whale are enemies, and yet they are brothers—

JOY

Brothers? Who says the Whale is a man? Always a man! What's wrong with a female whale? A Lesbian whale?

CHRIS

It's not! It's not! It's a great big strong hairy masculine whale and it's mine and you can't have it!

SONJA

The real money is in superconductors.

CHRIS

Well. So be it. I can see which way the wind is blowing. You've got the votes. You've got the demagogues and the rabble. You've got fire in the belly. The only thing is. . .

My chair is tenured.

He pulls the chair out from under Sonja. She falls. He sits. Music begins. They rise.

JOY

Wait!

They sit.

This just perpetuates itself. You can see where it's going. What are we doing here? There have to be alternatives. Here. Sit. We can both sit.

Slides over, offers half. Sonja stares.

It's ok.

KEVIN

Ok, she's offering, so sit.

CHRIS

Go ahead.

SONJA
I think I deserve it.

KEVIN
Sit.

SONJA
What's the catch?

JOY
Nothing. It's ok.

SONJA
She's doing that deliberately. Trying to make me feel guilty. Trying to say "Oh look how noble!" Well I don't feel guilty. This is as legitimately mine as anyone else's.

CHRIS
Go for it!

SONJA
Think I'm not gonna sit? Wrong! I'm gonna sit! I'm gonna sit like a ton of bricks!

ALL *(ad lib)*
Hey hey!

She bumps Joy off the chair. Sits. Music begins. Circulate. Stop. Scramble. Sonja is left standing.

KEVIN
Well say something. Don't just stand there.

CHRIS
She has a real attitude.

KEVIN
We are not excluding you because of your gender, race, religion, ethnicity, sexual orientation, or social class. It's purely a question of merit. You're just personally inferior.

CHRIS
Nothing personal.

KEVIN
There is a chair if she really wanted one.

CHRIS
The old saying, "You have to break eggs to make an omelette."

KEVIN *(to Sonja)*
I'll have an omelette, sweetie.

CHRIS
Break eggs the easy way: stomp on the hen!

They laugh. Stop. To Sonja:

Can't you take a joke?

Music. Final round between the two men, this time ruthless. Music stops. Kevin is left standing.

KEVIN

We've kinda whittled things down, haven't we? You know, this makes me think. I think we need to be more inclusive. If we had more of a mix. Like, Chris, all by yourself you're not really a mix. I know without all this total wasteland, we might not have so much prosperity.

But I mean, actually, Chris, are you the best we can do? I mean, I think our country is really in trouble if we exclude all the rich potentials of people like . . . me. You ever think what I might contribute? People I grew up with, places I've been— It's a whole world!

Like what if you never ate pizza, say, "Who'd want to eat a piece of flat pie smeared with ketchup!?" Ok, so never eat pizza. Never know those wonderful tastes and colors. My God, our natural resources: this crazy game has resulted in fewer chairs.

Do you ever think about getting to know each other? Value one another for uniqueness and we're not all alike and that's beautiful, and so what I'm trying to say is—

Clutching the chair leg, hysterically.

GIMME THE CHAIR, GIMME THE CHAIR, GIMME THE CHAIR!

He collapses, crawls off. Music begins. Chris clutches the chair legs, waddles about in a grotesque little dance. On the periphery, the group starts moving toward him. He stops. Looks around. Freeze. Fade.

Reach Out and Touch

A man enters, carrying a glass of milk, plate of food, fork and napkin. He speaks to us.

DAVIS

I started out very liberal. I answer my phone. My friends all monitor with their machines, but I did believe in being human. I'm in the minority.

He sits at the table. Says grace to himself. At a distance, the First Telemarketer punches button. Davis's phone rings. He gets up, answers it.

Hello?

FIRST

Hi, is this Randall Davies?

DAVIS

Davis.

FIRST

Mr. Davis, how you doing?

DAVIS

Fine.

FIRST

Mr. Davis, this is Kim from the Market Theatre. I'm calling because I notice your subscriptions are about to run out, and we'd like to have you renew them.

DAVIS

Well no, thanks, I don't think I will.

FIRST

For marketing reasons could I inquire why?

DAVIS

Well, my wife was very involved in the arts—

FIRST

Great—

DAVIS

But I'm not interested myself—

FIRST

Well perhaps I could speak—

DAVIS
And she passed away a few months ago.

FIRST
Oh. I'm so sorry. I mean—

DAVIS
It's not your fault, Kim. I get this every single day.

FIRST
No, I mean it's these lists, it's all computerized and— This is the third time— I think all their damn subscribers are dead. Oh I'm sorry, oh God, I mean— God, I hate selling things!

DAVIS
You sound like my daughter. Are you in college?

FIRST
No, I'm out of college, I'm just trying to— It's not really what I want to—

DAVIS
You have a degree in something?

FIRST
I got married before I got out of college.

DAVIS
Oh, you're married.

FIRST
I was.

DAVIS
Oh.

FIRST
I'm sorry. My supervisor's looking at me funny. Two minutes to a call.

DAVIS
That's ok. Bye.

FIRST
I'm sorry.

Hangs up.

I'm sorry, I'm sorry, I'm sorry!

Davis goes back to his meal. Second punches button. Phone rings. He answers.

DAVIS
Hello?

SECOND
Hi, Mr. Davison. This is Kathy from Country Fresh Farm. I wanted to let you know we have some representatives in your area this month. What we are is an all natural farm based in Lancaster, Pennsylvania, and operated by Amish. Have you ever heard of us?

DAVIS
Well no, actually—

SECOND
Am I catching you at a bad time?

DAVIS
Well, a lot of people eat dinner at dinnertime.

SECOND
I'm sorry. But actually it's kind of appropriate, because everyone's greatest concern is our health, and we here at Country Fresh Farm raise our meat completely organic. You may not know that most of the meat you eat is not pure but is loaded with steroids, antibiotics, sodium, preservatives, pesticides, artificial growth hormones—

DAVIS
Kathy— Actually my name is Davis, and right now I'm about to sit down to my steroids and pesticides, I've kinda been looking forward to'em.

SECOND
Well— What? But the other thing is that we deliver this meat right to your home every month, which you might consider how convenient this would be for your wife—

DAVIS
Kathy—

Third Telemarketer punches button.

I have another call. Could I put you on hold?

SECOND
Sure.

DAVIS
Hello?

THIRD
Dave! How are you!

DAVIS
Ok. Who's this?

THIRD
This is Fritz. How you doing tonight?

DAVIS
Eating my dinner.

THIRD
Great. Dave, I'm a representative of the Quadramatic Adjustable Bed Company. Can you hear me ok?

DAVIS
I've got another call—

THIRD
We got a postcard inquiring about our quality adjustable beds?

DAVIS
Oh, my wife sent that in, I think, she saw the ad, wondered what the price was—

THIRD
We don't talk price. For several reasons. First, our Quadramatic Adjustable Beds are cheaper than any quality flat bed, so if you need a bed to sleep on you're gonna pay the price. Second, we have many models, so what we would like to do is come to your home, sit down with you and your wife and discuss the features. For example the warming system, which is great for your lower back. Do you have any lower back pain, Dave?

DAVIS
Not in the back.

THIRD
How bout your wife?

DAVIS
She's peaceful.

THIRD
Great. So what we would like—

DAVIS
My wife is deceased.

THIRD
Sorry to hear that. We have many excellent single beds.

Davis hangs up.

Damn, I almost had him.

DAVIS *(back to call on hold)*
Kathy, sorry. Look, I don't think—

SECOND

I realize it's a bad time to call you, but our product, you can't buy it any way unless we call you, and it's a very important health concern— What I was going to ask, Mr. Davis, is how much meat do you eat a month?

DAVIS *(looking at his dinner)*

Not a whole lot right now.

SECOND

Well it's a very affordable program. We ship out every month in vacuum sealed bags, and it comes with a freezer, for free—

DAVIS

A freezer?

SECOND

A big freezer. We can sit down with you and—

DAVIS

So what, you're selling freezers?

SECOND

No, the freezer comes with the plan. The freezer is free. What we are selling is meat that is entirely organic, and raised by the Amish—

DAVIS

But the cost of the freezer is figured in, right?

SECOND

Well, we here at Country Fresh Farm are mainly concerned with the health aspects—

DAVIS

Kathy, listen, you're a nice girl. Be honest with me. You're selling meat and you're selling freezers.

SECOND

The freezer is free.

DAVIS

Think. It's not free. The price is included. Think.

SECOND

We're not sposed to.

DAVIS

Where is this farm in Lancaster County? I know Lancaster very well. Could you tell me where you're located?

SECOND

Uh . . . in the Amish area.

DAVIS
And are you using an Amish telephone?

SECOND
I'm not sure. I could find out—

DAVIS
Kathy. You sound like a nice person. Please tell your supervisor that not everyone you call is a driveling idiot. Goodbye.

He hangs up.

SECOND
I hate these people. I hate them. I hate them. I hate them.

Davis goes back to table. Halts, watching the phone. Nothing. Sits, starts to eat. It rings. He answers.

THIRD
Dave, Fritz again from Quadramatic. I wanted to call because I was thinking, maybe it's a good time to change beds, get rid of all those unpleasant memories.

DAVIS
Goodbye!

THIRD
Wait wait wait, LISTEN TO ME, NO MONEY DOWN!!!

Davis hangs up. Immediately another call.

DAVIS
Hello, this is Mr. Davis.

FOURTH *(obviously reading from a script)*
Mr. Davids, this is Tiffany. I'm calling you from Sunny Valley Memorial. Now that you are starting your new life with your lovely bride, we would like to help you look into the future. How are you today?

DAVIS
Look, you have the wrong information. We're not starting—

FOURTH
Many people don't like to think ahead, but your wife will want you to start preparing for the unexpected, and here at Sunny Valley—

DAVIS
Ok, you're selling funeral plots, and what I'm saying is, my wife is in fact deceased and is buried and so you can correct your records to reflect this.

FOURTH

You sure about that?

Pause. Davis tries to control himself.

DAVIS

Miss. I don't like to be impolite, but I have been on the phone to salespeople all night. My dinner wasn't much to start out with because I'm a lousy cook, but now it's stone cold, and so is my wife. Now one person tonight is going to listen to me, and that person is you.

Now I held her hand as she died. I held her hand and kissed her. I shared her last breath, and she is gone! From the face of the earth! She is not coming back to be buried in your damned cemetery!

FOURTH

Do you have a plot yourself?

He slams down the receiver. Stares at his food.

Center, the Telemarketers gather at vending machines, on break.

FIRST

Damn. They're out of Pepsi.

SECOND

Oh hey, you work for Richards, don't you?

FIRST

Cell 14.

SECOND

How is it there?

FIRST

I keep calling dead people.

SECOND

God, I know. . .

FIRST

And we have this great incentive. They fire two people every week. If you're one of the last two on the board, in terms of sales, you're gone.

SECOND

What I can't stand. . . You get the highest number of appointments in a day, you get to pop a balloon. They have this wall with balloons, five dollars in'em, ten dollars, a hundred dollars, and you pop a balloon. Why can't they just give you a bonus? "Daddy loves me. I get to pop a balloon." Then come home, sit down to supper, keep waiting for my husband to hang up on me.

FIRST
Mine just did.

THIRD
Hey, lighten up. You're paid to sell stuff. You're not paid to be an adult. You're not paid to be you.

SECOND
I don't think I should end every shift hating the people I talk to.

THIRD
Then do something else. Be a movie star. I'm just saying for your own good. Just accept the fact they hate you. Nothing personal.

FIRST
It's so divided. It's us against them. Get somebody on the phone, and maybe he just wants to talk. There are so many people that just want to talk.

THIRD
So talk. On your own time. Go home, open up the phone book, dial the phone and say, "Hi, I'm not selling nothing, I'm just a nice person. Would you like to talk?"

FIRST
That's not the point.

SECOND
So how do you feel at the end of the day?

THIRD
Crappy. How does the President feel?

SECOND
What about you?

FOURTH
I'm with Sunny Valley. I'm cool.

They return to their stations. Davis senses danger. Suddenly, all Telemarketers are calling simultaneously. His phone rings, he hangs it up, but it continues ringing as they talk simultaneously.

A new Telemarketer appears. Davis answers as others ad lib low in the background.

DAVIS
Hello!

FIFTH
Mr. Mavis?

DAVIS
Davis!

FIFTH
Are you the man of the house?

DAVIS
Yes!

FIFTH
Do you know there are ten million crimes in this country every week?

DAVIS
Great!

FIFTH
Do you feel safe in your home?

DAVIS
No!

FIFTH
Mr. Mavis, we're offering a special price on thirty issues of Guns & Ammo Magazine, would you be interested?

DAVIS
Guns & Ammo?

FIFTH
Guns & Ammo.

DAVIS
Guns & Ammo! Yes!

FIFTH
GOT'IM!

Blackout.

Evaluation

A woman sits in a chair, facing the audience. Throughout, she has no response whatever. Behind her, three actors — two male, one female, faced up-stage. At each sequence, two or three turn forward, focused on her — cradle to grave.

ONE
She just cries to get attention. Don't let her get away with it.

TWO
Well, I try to ignore it, but she just won't stop.

THREE
Maybe she'll be a politician. She's loud enough.

ONE
No, just a good wife and mother.

They turn upstage. Two forward: new characters.

THREE
Your daughter is very bright, but she's poorly motivated.

TWO
I was the same way. She's like me.

THREE
Also she has a low frequency of peer correlation.

TWO
What? She doesn't make friends?

Again.

THREE
One thing, she's got a nice personality.

ONE
Yeh, but she's on the Honor Roll, she writes poems, she's a brain.

THREE
She's not, once you get to know her.

ONE
What's the point of going out with somebody who isn't popular?

Again.

TWO
She's an excellent typist, follows orders, very efficient.

ONE
Communications skills?

TWO
She's not very warm on the telephone. Polite but dull.

ONE
I know the type.

Again.

THREE
She has no sense of reality. She wants kids right away.

ONE
I'll trade you wives any day of the week.

THREE
Oh, she's ok, but when we talk about money. . . She's just like her mother.

ONE
They're all alike.

Again.

TWO
She's spoiling those kids. She doesn't even try to control them.

THREE
They seem like nice kids.

TWO
They're noisy, they're always fighting, they run around in dirty clothes.

THREE
Some people just shouldn't have kids.

Again.

ONE
I walk in the door and she doesn't even say hello.

TWO
She makes you put up with a lot.

ONE
You're ten times the woman she is.

TWO
She doesn't deserve a guy like you.

Again.

THREE
She calls three, four times a week, "How's the kids, how's Kate?"

TWO
Why doesn't she join a club or something?

THREE
I try to ignore it, but she just won't stop.

TWO
She likes to feel sorry for herself.

Again.

ONE
Has she come to the dances before?

THREE
Why, you think she's cute?

ONE
She was dancing with that Stewart guy. Purple dress. Pitiful.

THREE
She'd dance with anything in pants.

Again.

ONE
Well she's lonely.

TWO
Ok, she's my mother, but she's just become impossible to manage, and I'm not going to keep on changing the sheets.

ONE
Lay down the law.

TWO
I think she does it on purpose, but she's getting too childish to realize it.

Again.

THREE
How much did she leave, you have any idea?

ONE
She wasn't worth all that much. She looks peaceful.

TWO
Nice funeral. Lots of flowers. Not many people.

THREE
Not that many people knew her that well.

Fade.

ALL-NIGHTER

In one area, J.J. sits by herself. During the scene, she remains alone, passes the time. In another area, Joy ushers in Chris and Susan.

JOY
Well about time.

CHRIS
Are we late?

JOY
Forty-five minutes ago you weren't.

CHRIS
What time we sposed to be here?

JOY
Twenty of, dummy.

CHRIS
Well we're here.

JOY
Where's Dave?

SUSAN
He's right behind us. He's parking.

JOY
Last night together!

CHRIS
Last night together. Where's the pizza?

JOY
It's on the way. Did you get popcorn? You get the stuff the bag goes in the micro and blows up?

SUSAN
I got three plain and one caramel.

CHRIS
Caramel! Let the good times roll!

JOY
Where's J.J.?

SUSAN
Isn't she here?

CHRIS
Announcing the Jack Nicholson film festival! I brought *The Shining*.

SUSAN
Five Easy Pieces.

Dave enters.

CHRIS
There's my man!

SUSAN
This is gonna be awesome.

JOY
So where's the rest of the troops? Didn't she come with you?

DAVE
Who? Oh, J.J. . . .

CHRIS
I talked to her machine. She'll be here.

JOY
Ok, here, I made up formal, whatcha call it, timetables?

DAVE
Bill of fare.

Dave takes a folded card from her, reads:

"Gang-of-Five-End-of-Exams-Senior-Year-Maybe-Last-Time-We'll-See-Each-Other-Till-Christmas All-Nighter." Gang of Five?

JOY
It had to sound official.

CHRIS *(reading)*
"Seven to eight p.m., snacks." We're in snacks?

JOY
We'll catch up.

CHRIS
"Bowling. Late night videos. Trivial Pursuit. Dawn breakfast at Friendly's." Hey, and the tape of our Quiz Bowl assembly?

All laugh.

DAVE
Comrades in arms!

SUSAN
Shot down in flames!

JOY
The sole and only thing I'll remember from high school.

CHRIS
Bounced from the assembly committee for conduct unbecoming.

SUSAN
The whole committee was bounced. You shoulda been the one to be bounced. It was your fault.

CHRIS
My fault? Hey, all I said was let's make it more interesting. I mean, every year, the Quiz Bowl, Parksburg High tradition, junior class nerds versus the senior class nerds. I just said, "Let's make the questions more interesting."

JOY
Yeh yeh, and we agreed.

DAVE
"Name the three top-rated drugs at Parksburg High."

SUSAN
"Who put the diddle in hey-diddle-diddle?"

JOY
"Which teacher would you least like to sleep with?"

Laughter.

CHRIS
"Which teacher *did* you least like to sleep with?"

SUSAN
That was a little much.

CHRIS
People loved it. The teachers loved it.

DAVE
Most of the teachers loved it. Some did not.

CHRIS
Some did not.

JOY
You guys, oh God, I'm gonna miss you!

To Chris:

Even you.

CHRIS
Me too.

After a moment:

DAVE

You guys are something else.

Pause. They look at him.

I can't get over it.

Laughs.

I never did tell you, anybody, how totally freaked I was. Of all of you. How do I say this? Here's me, dumb Polish working-class jock. *Second*-string jock. And I get stuck on this committee with the class genius *(indicating Chris)*, and weird J.J., doctor's kid, professor's kid *(indicating Susan)*, Miss Personality *(indicating Joy)*, people with *bookshelves* in their house, for Godsake. . .

Pause.

And you treated me like I was human. All these weird people. It really changed my life.

CHRIS

Isn't that special!

DAVE

Shut up!

Tussles with him, laughing.

JOY

So where *is* weird J.J.?

Pause. Changed tone:

DAVE

I don't think she's coming.

JOY

Huh?

DAVE

I called her, she said she's busy.

JOY

Come on. What? We talked about this for two months.

SUSAN

It was her idea.

JOY

I mean, we planned this. This is special. This was *planned!*

DAVE

I know—

JOY

One, I got a present for Eileen at Friendly's, for putting up with us for an entire year. She's on morning shift now. We've all gotta be there.

SUSAN

Well maybe she's—

JOY

And second, this bunch of weirdos has been very important to me, even the one I can't stand. *(poking Chris)* And I've got good news—

DAVE

Well what?

JOY

I want to wait for J.J.

Pause.

I love you guys!

CHRIS

Ok, so—

JOY

It's important to me!

CHRIS

We need some lightening up.

SUSAN

Should I put the popcorn in?

DAVE *(with an edge)*

You wanta tell some jokes?

CHRIS

Sure.

DAVE

I mean any jokes that don't demean somebody.

CHRIS

How can you have a joke that doesn't demean somebody?

SUSAN

He don't know the d'meaning of de word.

JOY *(to Chris)*

Oh, I meant to tell you. Remember that joke, you told that joke about the gay guy, with the eggplant? I told that to my acting class, they *died*, it was really funny!

CHRIS
Call for the pizza.

JOY
I called for the pizza.

DAVE
What's your opinion about it?

CHRIS
About what? The pizza? Pepperoni.

DAVE
Like about why J.J. isn't here.

CHRIS
Is this Quiz Bowl? J.J. with pepperoni, or J.J. with anchovies?

DAVE
Why do you think J.J.'s not here?

JOY
Why?

DAVE
I didn't realize she wasn't gonna come. I thought she was just— But she's just very offended by those jokes, Chris.

CHRIS
What?

DAVE
Your so-called jokes.

CHRIS
Whatta you talking about?

DAVE
Her brother's gay, and he came out to her parents, like two weeks ago, and a lot of stuff's coming down at home, and he flipped out, and. . .

Some of the stuff you said really hurt her.

JOY
It was really harmless, I mean. . . It was harmless.

DAVE
What if you got told a Jew joke? Say it's the Jew and the eggplant.

JOY
I think that's different.

DAVE
How?

JOY
I don't know. It's different. Jews don't do stuff with eggplants.

DAVE
What about jokes that *do* offend you?

CHRIS
People need a sense of humor.

SUSAN
Call her and apologize, Chris.

CHRIS
Why should I? I didn't mean anything. I don't even know her brother. I don't want to know her brother. He's a fag.

Others react.

That was a joke! Come on! She's gonna study Poly Sci. Sure, she'll meet a lot of really nice, sensitive, politically-correct people in politics. She better learn to take it.

DAVE
So jokes are stuff that somebody has to learn to take?

JOY
Call her up.

CHRIS
Hell no.

JOY
Then I will.

She gets up, goes to phone.

We're here to have a good time!

CHRIS
Somebody put the popcorn in?

JOY *(on phone)*
This is Joy. Could I speak with J.J.?

Pause. To others.

I mean I think it's really crappy. We've been planning for this.

In the other area, a young man appears.

MATTHEW
Phone.

J.J.
Who?

MATTHEW
Joy.

She makes a vague gesture. He goes.

CHRIS

It was a joke. I'm sorry if her family's freaked out. I'm aware there are a large number of emotionally unstable people out there, but that's not my fault. *(to Dave)* You puked on my foot in third grade: do I sit home and wipe my shoe?

Joy hangs up.

JOY

She's not there.

SUSAN

She's there.

JOY

I don't think Chris is to blame. It was a funny joke. I told it in class, everybody laughed.

CHRIS

The whole point of friends is you don't have to worry about what you say to'em. If she's my friend, she accepts me, and this is me. I accept her, but she doesn't accept me.

DAVE

That kind of stuff, Chris, it's like you're talking about people who aren't even human beings, this is not really a human being, this is a faggot, or a nigger, or a kike—

JOY

So we're supposed to treat her like something special? To me that's insulting her, like I don't think she's equal, like she's emotionally disturbed—

CHRIS

I don't see how it's going to promote cultural diversity and all that crap if we've always gotta think, "Oh her brother's gay, so no fag jokes, and oh, she's female, so no sex jokes, and maybe her mom's fat, so no elephant jokes."

What if it's my cultural heritage to tell gross, insulting jokes? Don't I have any rights? I don't have anything against gays. Put'em in the micro, maybe they'll pop.

Dead silence.

That's a joke, dammit!

DAVE

Chris, the best thing you ever did for me was to tell dumb jokes. I don't think there's anything wrong with jokes. Everything in'em, there's some kind of serious stuff. Everybody's ridiculous to think they're the only person with problems. And you'd make fun of me, and that was that good for me. "Lighten up, Dave."

CHRIS

Right, lighten up.

DAVE

You lighten up. You're going through the same dance you always did, but the music's changed. You're cruising around looking for somebody to beat up. I know it, Chris. I've been there.

CHRIS

Speak for yourself.

DAVE

Ok. I'm outa here.

JOY

Dave—

DAVE

I really don't feel into it right now. I'm sorry. . .

Goes out.

JOY

This is ridiculous!

SUSAN *(getting up)*

Me too.

JOY

Susan—

Knock at door. Joy goes.

Pizza.

CHRIS *(to Susan)*

Stay and eat the pizza.

SUSAN

I just—

Pizza Kid comes in following Joy.

JOY

How much?

PIZZA KID

Twenty-six bucks.

Joy figures the tip, counts out money. He looks around at the others. She pays.

PIZZA KID
Somebody die here or something?

He goes out. Joy stacks the pizza boxes on the table. Silence. Dave returns.

DAVE
I forgot my coat.

JOY
Have some pizza.

SUSAN
This half's with anchovies, Dave. You like that.

DAVE
I just came back to get my coat.

He stands motionless. In the other area, Matthew appears at the door. J.J. looks up, goes to him and takes his hand.

JOY
All I feel is, if she chooses not to come, why that's her choice. She's the one excluding herself, and I feel like she's being unfair to me and the rest of us by being so super-sensitive, and that's all I have to say.

SUSAN *(to Dave)*
Did you bring *Easy Rider*?

DAVE
Chinatown.

CHRIS
Dave. . .

In other area, Matthew goes out. J.J. sits again, picks up a book. Dave sits down, opens the box.

DAVE
Eat the pizza.

Fade.

CEREMONIES IN CONCRETE

A young African-American Man, in suit and tie, enters, takes out a roll of masking tape, begins taping out a square on the sidewalk.

Store Owner appears, watching him. When he finishes taping, he stands in the square and does absolutely nothing.

STORE OWNER

Hi. 'Lo there. What's that?

Silence.

Oh yeh. it's a square, ain't it? You taped out a square on the sidewalk. Well, it's a nice day for it. No more snow.

Silence.

Say, you know, we're trying to do business here, and you're standing in front of my store. You got a permit?

Silence. Mabel appears, in cloth coat and stocking cap, carrying packages. She passes, stops, stares. A Young Woman stops.

Hey come on, I'm trying to reason with you. This is a free country, so buzz off.

YOUNG WOMAN

What is he doing?

STORE OWNER

Hey!

Waves hands in front of Man's eyes. No response.

YOUNG WOMAN

Excuse me. Who is sponsoring this?

STORE OWNER

This guy he just tapes out a square on the sidewalk and he won't say anything.

YOUNG WOMAN

He's just standing there.

STORE OWNER

Lady, I am in business here, my father was in business here. What are you, Mother Teresa?

YOUNG WOMAN
No I work in public relations—

STORE OWNER
He can go to a shelter.

YOUNG WOMAN
He's not homeless. He's wearing a suit and tie.

STORE OWNER
So he comes from a good family. Look, guy. I'm not prejudiced against you. I'll prove it. Here's a buck. Scram.

MABEL *(suddenly breaking her stare)*
You doing a survey? Listen, young man, if you're doing a survey I can help you out, cause I got a lot of opinions. You probably seen me in the newspapers, in the letters to the goddamned editor, I always sign it "Disgusted on Walnut Street."

YOUNG WOMAN
Free speech. He's exercising his right to free speech.

STORE OWNER
He won't speak! I'm gonna peel up the damn tape.

MABEL
Look out. It might be that supermarket tape. It's radioactive, see. They mark things when they're on sale so you won't buy'em, and the cash register reads this tape because it's radioactive, and your hair falls out.

STORE OWNER
Huh?

MABEL
Yeh, my sister-in-law. She got this tape, you stick it on your face every night, see, and your face grows into a smile.

STORE OWNER
So?

MABEL
She lost three cats.

STORE OWNER
Pull up the tape!

YOUNG WOMAN
Wait. I'll talk to him. I'm in public relations. Sir, hi. You know, I couldn't help noticing that you were standing there, in what seems to be a taped-out box on the sidewalk, and you seem to be standing in it, and we were all wondering . . . Why?

Silence.

He doesn't answer.

STORE OWNER

No kidding.

YOUNG WOMAN

He must be deaf or he'd answer.

STORE OWNER

Are you deaf? ARE YOU DEAF?

YOUNG WOMAN

No, wait. I see. This is art. A sidewalk artist.

STORE OWNER

Art.

YOUNG WOMAN

There was a man who got a lot of money to walk around in a big paper bag. And I said to my husband, "Well that's his bag."

MABEL

Oh yeh. And my cousin, she married this guy, he'd go out on the street, he'd jump around, see, and then when he got a whole crowd, he'd expose himself. Cause he'd get a big laugh.

YOUNG WOMAN

That's it. This is an expression of his alienation. Or his search for his roots. Or— *(to the man)* But maybe you could explain to me: This is a square box. I would have thought perhaps a round box would feel more . . . tribal.

STORE OWNER

Look, I don't want any trouble, guy. If you're getting ready to riot—

YOUNG WOMAN

You know I sympathize with what you represent. If you would be a little more specific about what you represent.

STORE OWNER

Give'em an inch, they take a mile.

YOUNG WOMAN

You do represent something, don't you? You can't really justify standing there unless you represent something.

STORE OWNER

He's just a punk.

YOUNG WOMAN

Sir, are you a punk? Please tell us. I really am in a hurry.

MABEL

Is he that celebrity where they made a big stink about him killing his wife? I never could see what was so great about that show. I got tired of it.

STORE OWNER

So if you're a celebrity, so tap-dance.

MABEL

Like before, they were always talking about the Communists. Nothing but Communist this, Communist that. You got sick of it. And then old Saddam Hussein, he was big a while, and then they cancelled him. Pretty soon you'll get the Communists coming back. As a series.

YOUNG WOMAN

You know, art has to communicate.

STORE OWNER

I worked for everything I got! That's my store! Not yours! You can't have it! It's mine!

MABEL

I'm ready to throw it out the window.

STORE OWNER

Listen creep! Let's lay it on the line! I was in the Marines. Six months in the Marines. There's people fighting and dying right now to keep this sidewalk free.

Starts to advance. A woman appears: a Lawyer.

LAWYER

What is this? Why are you harassing this man?

STORE OWNER

Harassing? He's dragging down the neighborhood—

YOUNG WOMAN

We're waiting for him to tap-dance.

LAWYER

I'm advising you that I am an attorney and I do a great deal of litigation on civil rights. So hands off!

STORE OWNER

Is this a protest?

YOUNG WOMAN

That's what it is. A stand-in.

LAWYER

Listen, brother. I sympathize. But can we talk about this? You have to realize that everything you do is political. Everything makes a statement. We must choose our tactics very carefully.

YOUNG WOMAN
If this is a protest, why don't you offer some constructive alternatives?

LAWYER
See, to you you are saying, "I want my identity! I want my heritage! I want my piece of the action!" But the media will play this up as Separatism. Like "He wants his little box on the sidewalk? Fine. We'll take the rest of the sidewalk."

YOUNG WOMAN
We have tried to include you, and this is our thanks.

MABEL
What the Arabs are doing, they got these plans. They buy it all up, put parking lots all over. They put all these parking lots up, and then when we park there, they close'em, and all over America we gotta take the bus.

LAWYER
So here you are, standing there. What about your brothers and sisters who are homeless? They are stereotyping you and co-opting you and you are playing into their hands.

YOUNG WOMAN
This man has decided to protest, right here on city property. Probably something about racism, violence, poverty — everything we believe in.

STORE OWNER
Do you realize, fella, that this sidewalk belongs to the taxpayers? I'm a taxpayer.

YOUNG WOMAN
So am I.

LAWYER
I take allowable deductions.

MABEL
I cheat.

STORE OWNER
You may think you own this sidewalk but it's as much mine as yours, probably more—

MABEL
Tell'im.

STORE OWNER

I'm gonna show you I have as much right to that square as you do, probably more—

MABEL

Show'im.

YOUNG WOMAN

Go on. Show him.

LAWYER

Yes!

Store Owner dramatically puts his foot down inside the square.

STORE OWNER

HAH!

Pause, then a mass outburst of energy.

Let's go, Gyrenes!

YOUNG WOMAN

All together now!

LAWYER

Equal access!

MABEL

Action!

All shove into the square, ejecting the man. Ad lib.

STORE OWNER

We showed him!

MABEL

What a pushover!

YOUNG WOMAN

Enough is enough.

All are jammed together inside the square.

MABEL

My name's McClafferty.

YOUNG WOMAN

Glad to meet you. I'm Tracey.

STORE OWNER

Sam.

LAWYER

Bornstein, Rutledge & Cooper.

As they continue, the man goes about six feet away and starts taping out another square.

MABEL
That's two f's in McClafferty, if you wanta know, which most people don't cause they don't give a damn about nothing these days pardon my language but it's a fact.

YOUNG WOMAN
Well. Small world.

STORE OWNER
Is that something? We all get together we can really get this country moving again.

LAWYER
Do you people do this all the time?

YOUNG WOMAN
Isn't this great? We all come together, and get to know each other's cultures, and lifestyles, and recipes—

MABEL
No smoking if you please!

YOUNG WOMAN
It's so wonderful when people come together.

LAWYER
Someone is standing on my foot!

They see the man standing in the new square.

YOUNG WOMAN
Look.

LAWYER
He's doing it again.

STORE OWNER
Dammit, he's doing it again.

LAWYER
Stop that, do you hear me? Your actions reflect on me!

MABEL
That's a man for you.

YOUNG WOMAN
Maybe we hurt his feelings. There's room for all kinds. Invite him back in.

STORE OWNER
You kidding?

YOUNG WOMAN

We excluded him. *(to Lawyer)* And you must feel out of place, being a minority. He'll be company for you.

LAWYER

Actually I don't need a lot more company right now.

YOUNG WOMAN

Look, there's plenty of room. We're sorry.

MABEL

He's not the sociable type. Like my niece's husband, he sits in the bathroom all day.

YOUNG WOMAN

It is rather stuffy here. Do we all want to bunch up like this? There's lots of room on the sidewalk.

STORE OWNER

I had to push to get in here. I'm not giving it up now.

LAWYER

This is symbolic.

MABEL

Don't squeeze the packages. I save these for the post office to smash.

YOUNG WOMAN

I always stand in the wrong line.

STORE OWNER

Listen, I'm not much for politics. But this has to mean something. This is where all the little guys — ok, all the little gals too — where we took a stand. We cannot have died in vain.

MABEL

There's this video game where if you have gaps it all runs out.

LAWYER

I think I may be sick.

All shuffle around, trying to avoid the possibility.

YOUNG WOMAN

Wait. I have an idea. The tape.

STORE OWNER

Tape?

YOUNG WOMAN

If we had his tape we could make our own boxes.

STORE OWNER

Branch out.

LAWYER
A subdivision.

MABEL
Condominiums.

YOUNG WOMAN
Ask to borrow the tape.

LAWYER
Don't ask. Demand!

STORE OWNER
Excuse me sir, I wonder if you might lend us that tape. . . Please, may we borrow your tape? . . . You suppose we might use that tape there?

LAWYER *(exploding)*
Give us the mother-loving tape!

YOUNG WOMAN
You antagonized him! Wait. I have another plan.

MABEL
Operation Here-We-Go-Again.

They huddle together, mumble, each pointing different directions. Then they rotate till the Store Owner is across from the Man. Others hold him by the belt, tilt him out at a 45-degree angle toward the Man. Store Owner extends his hand, cordially.

STORE OWNER
Hi there. Now give us that tape. Please give us the tape. Please. Tape. GIVE US THE TAPE YOU SON OF A BITCH!!!—

All ad lib. He flails wildly, trying to reach Man. At last finds himself clutching the lapel of a Cop.

YOUNG WOMAN
Oh, Officer, I'm glad you're here, I—

COP
What's cooking?

STORE OWNER
This creep was standing here and—

COP
Come on, sing.

LAWYER
Officer, he was standing here in pursuit of his own personal beliefs which I respect but which I do not condone—

COP

I heard it all before, sister.

LAWYER

And you will be held responsible for any assault and battery committed on him while I am present but I am now leaving.

Goes.

COP

I give you all a count of five. Onetwothreefive. That's all she wrote.

YOUNG WOMAN

I have another meeting. Bye-bye.

MABEL

Well, if you're on one of those cop shows you should tell'em not to drive around so much. But so, I got official business with the United States government to mail these packages. This is for my cousin in Sheboygan, she still celebrates Reagan's birthday, only she don't know when it is cause they kept it a secret so the Russians wouldn't screw it up. It's a blender. You put your garbage in there and it makes a milk shake.

She goes off. Cop looks at Store Owner.

STORE OWNER

See, this is my store over here, and this guy was—

COP

Don't you have to go potty or something?

STORE OWNER

Yes. Thank you.

He goes. Cop looks at Man standing.

COP

Loading zone.

Takes out chalk, marks his shoe. Stands, timing with wristwatch. Man goes. Cop looks at box. Considers. Stands in the box. Blackout.

ROOMMATES

College dormitory room. Jed, 21, an African-American college student, professional class background. Ric, 20, a Polish-American college student, working class background. Jed moves about in a rush to organize notebooks, other things to go out. Ric enters.

JED

Ric, can you get those socks out of the corner? They're growing there.

RIC

Sure.

JED

They're starting to be a new form of biology. Term project in biology.

RIC

I'll take care of'em.

Comes in, sits on bed.

Where you going?

JED

I have to go to a meeting. Ten minutes ago.

RIC

You're never on time.

JED

We have Colored Peoples' Time. This is similar to Polish time, Jewish peoples' time, Italians' time, anybody's time that's never on time. But I on the other hand keep my socks out of the corner.

RIC

I'll do the socks!

Pause.

JED

Did we just have a— What would you call it? Difference? Disputation? Dissonance?

RIC

I'm sorry. I'm very. . .

JED
Oh. Letter from home? One of those?

RIC
One of those.

JED
Wanta talk?

RIC
You're late.

JED
They know me.

RIC
What is it?

JED
Just some people.

RIC
Well.

JED
Hey. We friends? Co-conspirators?

RIC
Of what?

JED
Well we keep each other's dark secrets. So nobody in this elite institution suspects. That I a Nee-gro and you a redneck.

RIC
Well I wear high collars.

JED
And I wear a smiiiiiiiile!

Laugh. Then silence.

RIC
I shouldn't be here. I should be back in the community college preparing to be an alcoholic. What the hell am I doing here?

JED
You're escaping your sleazy past.

RIC
It's my family. Ok, it's a sleazy family, they'll never be on TV, but they're mine. I'm sposed to forget that?

JED
Don't you want to?

RIC

Yes! No! Oh hell, it's just a different world. It's hard to associate with all these little doctor's kids and lawyer's kids and then get a letter from my sister—

My dad's a beer alcoholic. Not gin and tonic. Not martinis. You know how dedicated you have to be to get wasted on beer every day?

JED

Ric. Why are you here?

RIC

College education.

JED

You're here to get a ticket into that different world, right? There are people who do their wash in the laundromat, and people who don't. Your ambition is to be one of the Don'ts.

RIC

Sit in Sociology, they talk about poor people, they talk about ghettos, everybody looks over at you.

JED *(laughing)*

My daddy the ghetto neurosurgeon.

RIC

If I spoke up and said, "Hey you wanta hear about trying to get the landlord to stop rats running across my little brother's bed?" Kelly says, "Why don't you join a fraternity?" "Because I can't afford it, baby!"

JED

And I get flak at the BSU for being in a fraternity. "You can't be a brother if you a *brother*." "What, you tryin pretend you White?" "Yes, yes, I am! That's what I'm here for! That's what I'm majoring in! Caucasian Studies! That's where the money's at!"

They laugh. Then silence.

Hey, I don't like to leave you suicidal.

RIC

Never mind. I got half the 19th Century to study. That'll cheer me up.

JED

Please play that boring music while I'm gone so I don't have to hear it when I get back.

RIC
And do my socks.

JED
And do your socks.

RIC
Where to?

JED
Meeting.

RIC
What meeting?

JED
Lambda.

RIC
Lambda.

JED
Yeh.

RIC
How come you're goin to Lambda?

JED
It's a good bunch.

RIC
I mean, are you talking about . . . the gay . . . group? They don't even publicize where they meet.

JED
Well on this campus. I mean you don't advertise, right?

RIC
Yeh but— I mean you just did—

Silence.

I mean are you telling me—?

JED
Well we're friends. If you were into hang-gliding, I expect you'd mention it at one time or another—

RIC
I don't hang-glide.

JED
I don't hold it against you.

RIC
Jesus, Jed— Are you kidding?

JED
Hey! Is this a big thing?

RIC
No— Yeh— No— Ok, what you do is up to you—

JED
Thanks—

RIC
But I mean— Are you seeing anybody?

JED
Seeing— I have a couple of friends—

RIC
No, I mean— Like a therapist?

JED
Therapist?

RIC
I don't mean you're sick, I mean it might help some adjustment or something—

JED
I'm adjusted. I think I'm adjusted as I can be in this atmosphere.

RIC
Look, no, Jed— Are we friends?

JED
I think so. I hope to God so—

RIC
How long have we known each other? Two years?

JED
Two and a half. Yes. I know. Why didn't I say something? Why the hell do you think? Isn't it obvious? I was afraid of some kind of reaction like this.

RIC
What, I'm not sposed to react— You just drop this on me—

JED
All right, so I get a C-. Let me hand in a rewrite. I know. It takes some getting used to. You worked very hard on the race thing, and I know you went through some frenzied discussion with your mother when she found out you were rooming with One Of Those. And it's not really fair to have to two serious character flaws, being black and being gay, pardon the expression, I mean let's not mix up our cultural minorities—

RIC
You went out with Doreen—

JED
Doreen's gay. Well, sort of bisexual maybe. Actually, she's something that hasn't been invented yet.

RIC
You're crazy.

JED
No.

RIC
Doreen's Catholic.

JED
So it gives her something to confess. Look, I'm sorry, ok? I guess I tried to say something very casual, because we're friends and I don't think it's friends to conceal a whole aspect of life, ok? And I thought maybe you'd just think, "Oh, well I didn't know that. That's interesting."

RIC
Look, no— I'm just really concerned. What if it gets on your record? Some grad school, or corporation, "Well he was vice president of Lambda? What's Lambda? Oooh."

JED
Let me worry about—

RIC
Your fraternity—

JED
I don't intend to—

RIC
And how many little wisecracks are you gonna just barely overhear? And one of these days you just can't restrain yourself and you say "Hey, I'm gay!" And then it hits the fan.

JED
This is the 21st Century!

RIC
Not around here!

JED
Half-overheard comments. Or trying to smile at the great jokes? "How many faggots does it take to screw in a Polack?" Haw haw haw!

RIC
It was actually funnier than that.

JED
I missed the subtleties.

RIC
What about AIDS?

JED
What about it?

RIC
Well just—

JED
I don't have it, sorry. Hey Ric, what about syphilis? You got syphilis? Will you please give me a break! Right now any guy that I know is less likely to get AIDS than 95% of the straights on this campus who would hump anything that's lying in the street. Come on.

Pause.

Is what you're worried about is somebody finding out and thinking about you being my roommate?

RIC
No. Hell. Come on.

JED
I'm not carrying a flag.

RIC
I don't care what people think.

JED
Ok.

RIC
As long as my parents don't know.

JED
Ok.

RIC
I don't see how they could.

JED
I wouldn't think.

RIC
So no problem.

JED
No problem. So what's the problem?

RIC
Look, it's your own life, but— Don't you have to go to your meeting?

JED
This is what my meeting is all about!

Pause. Both try to calm down.

Ok, are we going to debate morality now, because if that's it then I'd rather we meet at dawn with big heavy Bibles at ten paces.

RIC
I think people are free to do what they want. I also think there are some things, that for the good of society, society disapproves. And you can't blame people if they subscribe to that.

JED
Such as, let's see, "What if everybody was gay?" Although that's never seemed very likely. I'm hip to gay pride and black pride and all the other prides, but I don't think we've necessarily got something so special going for us that the entire human race is gonna come knocking and say "Can we join the party?" I wouldn't worry about that.

Pause.

So what is it? You think I might come on to you?

RIC
No.

JED
Will you please not worry? There are people you find attractive and others you don't? Right?

RIC
Right.

JED
Karen is very attractive. To most people. Actually to anybody. Actually to me. Whereas Maryanne Felcher is not.

RIC
Very much not.

JED
You could sleep in the same bed as her and you'd both get a good night's sleep.

RIC
Definite.

JED
Although she might be a firecracker.

RIC
All things are possible.

JED
So don't worry.

RIC
In what sense?

JED
I don't find you attractive.

RIC
Oh. You don't.

JED
No I don't.

RIC
Find me attractive.

JED
I do not.

RIC
Why the hell you think I want you to find me attractive?

JED
That wasn't my point. I was saying not to worry. To me. I mean maybe to somebody else.

RIC
Right.

JED
Have no fear. You can swing from the light fixture naked.

Pause. Ric turns toward his desk, back to Jed, opens a book.

What's the matter?

RIC
What's so repulsive about me?

JED
Nothing. I'm just saying—

RIC
Saying I'm a loser.

JED
No.

RIC
I don't give a damn what you think—

JED
I'm expressing—

RIC
Ok!

JED
If it bothers you so much then we could change roommates. People do all the time.

RIC
Maybe.

JED
Maybe we spend too much time together.

RIC
Maybe.

JED
Maybe I should have kept my mouth shut.

RIC
Maybe.

JED
Ric? Are *you* gay?

Pause. They look at one another.

RIC
Well no, actually I'm not. I guess that'd be a neat surprise. But I'm just damned depressed and I've got my own problems and I don't need yours. So I'd just appreciate it if you keep your nose out of my business and let me worry about my own problems and not think you—

Goddamn it, you're the only friend I've got here, what the hell right do you— Look, you can't help being black, but can't you— I mean—

Pause. He's totally tangled up.

These are the Wonder Years.

Pause.

Jed. You're my friend. Before anything else you're my friend. I need a friend. Be my friend.

JED
I will do my best.

RIC

I'm sorry.

JED

Ok.

RIC

Look, please—

JED

No problem.

Pause. He tries to lighten it with a joke.

As long as you get those socks out of the corner!

It falls flat.

We've got some territory to cover.

RIC

Give it time.

They sit, looking at one another. Fade.

DINNER PARTY

Two men, with drinks, sit in a living room. They mirror each other's gestures. They talk alike. They're dressed alike. They're named George.

GEORGE 1
Good to see you, George.

GEORGE 2
Good to see you too.

GEORGE 1
You're looking good.

GEORGE 2
You too.

GEORGE 1
Looking just like me.

GEORGE 2
Well it's nice to look like each other. No surprises.

GEORGE 1
How's the wife?

GEORGE 2
Just like yours.

GEORGE 1
I should think of a sex joke here.

GEORGE 2
Me too. Well, the usual crude comments. And then we laugh.

They laugh. Then they stop, embarrassed.

That felt pretty dumb.

GEORGE 1
I know. But I won't say so.

GEORGE 2
Me neither.

GEORGE 1
George, frankly, aren't you bored silly?

GEORGE 2
Well I try to. It's not easy. Tell you what, George, since we don't have anything to say to each other, let's make conversation.

GEORGE 1
Good idea, George. Get it out of the way.

GEORGE 2
Let's see. What do you think about minorities?

GEORGE 1
I think they must be that way for a reason.

GEORGE 2
Good point. They do kinda bother me.

GEORGE 1
They bother me too, George. It's nothing personal. I just wish they'd all die.

GEORGE 2
Except for the good ones. There are exceptions. We have to be fair-minded.

GEORGE 1
I'm afraid we do. Well that's one topic out of the way.

GEORGE 2
I guess it's time for our wives to come in and do some chitchat so we don't have to communicate.

Two women enter, kiss their husbands, and sit.

GEORGINA 1
Hi guys.

GEORGINA 2
We were just doing some chitchat out there. Boy, your wife is a real dum-dum.

GEORGE 1
Well that's what attracted me. But it's boring as hell.

GEORGINA 1
We thought about saving up for a divorce.

GEORGE 1
Kind of an anniversary present. But it's expensive.

GEORGE 2
Have you checked the new Japanese lawyers? Very economical.

GEORGE 1
Where's what's-their-names?

GEORGINA 1
I forgot. It's hard to remember they're here when they're here.

A third couple enter, wave, sit.

GEORGE 3
Surprise. We were waiting out there so we wouldn't have to come in here and bc bored.

GEORGINA 3
Good to see you.

GEORGE 1
Let's see, you all know one another? George and Georgina, George, Georgina.

GEORGE 3
And George and. . .

GEORGINA 3
Georgina. Hi.

GEORGE 1
Well, good, now you're here we can tell some dumb jokes.

GEORGE 2
I love it.

GEORGE 3
I heard this one. Ok. Three guys, a white guy and a Negro and a Jew are walking along the beach— This is multicultural, nobody here's multicultural, right?

GEORGE 2
No problem—

GEORGE 3
So the Negro says, "I wonder how deep the ocean is." And the Jew says, "You're so dumb you must be a Negro." To which the white guy says, "Look who's talking."

Dead silence.

GEORGINA 2
That's a funny one.

They all laugh. Then stop.

GEORGE 2
I've got one. There's a husband and a wife. The wife is being a real bitch. The husband says, "You must have PMS."

Dead pause. Brief laugh.

GEORGE 1
Hey! If it takes ten Polacks to change a light bulb, what do they do when they're finished?

They laugh uproariously..

GEORGINA 3
What do you call a homosexual man if you want to insult him? A faggot!

Dead silence.

GEORGE 3
You didn't tell it right.

GEORGINA 3
That's the way I heard it.

GEORGE 2
Ok, this is great. What do fraternity guys drink at parties? Fraternity guys at parties?

GEORGINA 2
I give up.

GEORGE 3
Beer.

They laugh wildly, at length, then stop, dismal.

GEORGINA 2
Are we done with that?

GEORGE 1
Sounds like it. Well. Sports. Who are your favorite teams?

GEORGE 2
I root for the winners.

GEORGE 3
Same here.

GEORGE 1
Great. Well. College days.

GEORGE 2
Those were great days.

GEORGE 3
Same here.

GEORGE 1
Except for the apathy.

GEORGE 3
Same here.

GEORGINA 2
Well the main value of college is is to separate the sheep from the goats.

GEORGE 2
You're right about that. Are you a sheep or a goat?

GEORGINA 2
Sheep.

GEORGE 3
Sheep.

GEORGINA 1
Definitely a sheep.

GEORGINA 3
Count me in.

GEORGE 1
Yes sir, yes sir, three bags full.

Dead pause.

GEORGINA 1
I always dread having to get through an evening with you people.

GEORGE 3
Same here.

GEORGINA 2
It's really special.

GEORGINA 1
I mean it's interesting how we start out so different, backgrounds and ideas and feelings, you see little children on the playground, and then gradually we sort of blend together so we're all interchangeable and employable. Sometimes it makes me want to run off and have an affair.

GEORGINA 3
Well I did. But he was totally boring.

GEORGE 3
I think in fact that was me. We didn't recognize each other.

GEORGINA 3
Oh was that you? No wonder.

GEORGINA 2
I wonder if dinner's ready.

GEORGE 2
Whose house are we at?

GEORGE 1
I think it's yours, isn't it?

GEORGE 3
No, there's a stain on our sofa.

GEORGE 2
There's one on ours too.

GEORGE 3
Well ours is sort of kidney shaped.

GEORGE 1
No I guess this is our house, cause I don't remember getting in the car.

GEORGINA 1
And I remember putting something in the oven. I wouldn't have put something in somebody else's oven.

GEORGE 1
Isn't that something! We're right at home! Well! What's for appetizers?

GEORGINA 1
Baba ghanouj.

Dead silence.

I mean— Is that ok? I mean— I don't want to offend anybody, or—

GEORGINA 2
Sure, I mean—

GEORGE 3
If that's—

GEORGINA 1
Hey— I'm not pushing affirmative action or alternative lifestyles or something. I just like different kinds of foods.

GEORGE 1
Jeez, honey, you can't just put our whole private life out there in front of total strangers.

GEORGINA 1
It's our best friends.

GEORGE 1
Same thing.

GEORGINA 1
Well I have some pork chops—

GEORGINA 2
Ratatouille.

GEORGINA 1 *(shocked)*
You do ratatouille?

GEORGINA 2
Yes I do.

GEORGE 2
Hon, some things are personal.

GEORGINA 3
Falafal. Moussaka. Kolokithokeftedes.

GEORGINA 1
What?!

GEORGINA 3
Little pumpkin patties.

The women become more and more enthusiastic, the men increasingly embarrassed.

GEORGE 1
Hey, you guys have some kind of a . . . secret life, hey?

GEORGE 3
Well no, not as a regular thing. I mean maybe once in a while, just for the variety—

GEORGINA 1
Gnocci. Calzone. Funghi ripieni. Fritto misto.

GEORGINA 2
Tortellini.

GEORGINA 3
Cannelloni. Capellini. Pappadelle. Linguini—

GEORGE 3
Sometimes a pizza.

GEORGE 2
Hey. You don't have to hide it from us. We're broad-minded.

GEORGE 1
Actually some of the more kinky stuff, it makes you appreciate good old steak and potatoes.

GEORGINA 1
Bliny. Vatrushky. Babka yablochnaya—

GEORGINA 2
I don't know that.

GEORGINA 1
Try it, you'll die!

GEORGE 1
I mean it isn't like we were swingers or something—

GEORGINA 3
How did you get started?

GEORGINA 1

It was him, actually. He came home from a business trip, and he left his briefcase unlocked, and I found a knish.

GEORGE 1

And we talked it over, and she agreed to try it, and it's really brought us closer together.

GEORGINA 2

Knishes. Latkes. Blintzes.

GEORGINA 3

Tsimmes. Gefilte fish.

GEORGINA 1

I mean there are a few things we're not quite ready for—

GEORGINA 2

Chitlins. Kele wele. Gado-gado.

GEORGINA 3

Bouillabaisse. Vichyssoise. Borscht.

GEORGINA 1

Ojojo! *(explaining)* Yam fritters.

Alternately, then in duos and trios, then in unison, the six begin chant-and-response, a gastronomic litany of discovery. The parts are to be divided and orchestrated. At last, they move into a round dance.

ALL

Jajik. Givech. Strudel. Kasha. Tamales. Burritos. Tacos. Enchiladas. Frijoles. Grits. Fasnacht. Shteepers. Scrapple. Khoya. Chapatis. Oshi tashi. Yow bing. Hang yang wu. Sushi. Teriyake. Dombai. Tiropetes. Keftedakia. Shish kebab. Katemeria. Dizi. Kulebiaka. Pirozhki. Botvinia. Karnabeet makly. Salatet malfoof. Kalamarakia tighanita. Fool midammis.

GEORGINA 1

Singgang ajam. It's great. You pound it with a mallet.

ALL

Rassolnik. Spas. Gutap. Pashtet. Ukha. Yaini. Kurnik. Tabaka. Tkemali. Kotmis satsivi. Churek. Ghalva. Blumenkohlsuppe. Biersuppe. Heilbutt. Kalbshaxe. Sauerbraten. Wuerzfleisch. Hasenpfeffer. Kartoffelpuffer. Hoppelpoppel. Mtori.

GEORGINA 2

Omigod. Africa! Africa!

ALL

Samaki kavu. Bobitie. Fufu. Kitfo. Mokoto. Tere sega. Doro wat. Gari foto. Geelrys. Niter kebbeh. Aboloo. Bolo polana. Chippolata. Cocada amarela.

The litany has built to a fever pitch. All feel the spirit, love and joy reigning. Sudden change: quiet and lyrical, with music.

GEORGE 1

You know maybe I'm out of line on this, but— Is it too crazy to think that— I don't mean to sound socialist or something, but—

See, like here we are, and there's something we all share, and sure, it's not something we want to advertise, maybe, but see, even if it's only going from Taco Bell to Pizza Hut, there's a tuning into the whole incredible richness of human beings, and if we can taste somebody else's food, maybe tomorrow we can listen to his music, and then hear what he has to say, and then look him in the face, and it won't be that difficult, or scary—

It might be stimulating— And productive— And fun! Fun! Real fun! Real love and peace and family and joy and—

Looks around, embarrassed.

Not to take away from good old steak and potatoes.

The sextet goes into barbershop harmony, then into recitative, building to a climactic shout.

ALL

Minestrone. Caponata. Ravioli. Pollo al diavolo. Pollo alla cacciatore. Pollo con pepperoni. Farsu magru. Osso buco. Beer cheese. Fried grits. Scrambled brains! Hush puppies!! Fortune cookies!!!

Silence. They look at one another. Very quietly:

GEORGINA 2

There's a whole world out there.

And they fade into history.

Just Coffee

Coffee shop. Two sisters. Waitress takes order.

CARRIE
Just coffee.

SARA
Two coffees.

Waitress goes off.

Oh God, Carrie, it's so good to see you. I've really needed to talk, and you're busy or I'm busy, or—

Well here we are.

CARRIE
Here we are.

She takes Sara's hand. They hold hands a moment, smiling.

SARA
Well. I had a terrible fight with Mom.

CARRIE
About Jerry?

SARA
The closer it gets to the wedding—

CARRIE
Yeh—

SARA
Well you know it's race. She doesn't want to say it is. But it is.

CARRIE
It's not easy for her.

SARA
She tells me, "You're gonna have problems." I say, "Ok, so don't you be one of'em."

CARRIE
It's a different generation.

SARA
She gets onto kids. "What's he gonna be, black or white? Who will he identify with?" "People with brains in their heads and love in their hearts."

So ok, so maybe he, she would be better off if his parents were rich, and everybody all lived in 1955, and there's no history of diabetes in my family.

But the best thing I can do for a child of mine is give him Jerry for a father, and if that makes him come out the wrong shade, then so be it.

CARRIE
So are you thinking about having kids?

SARA
That's often what married people do.

Pause. Waitress brings coffee. They are silent as she serves it. Waitress goes.

Carrie?

CARRIE
Well it's none of my business.

SARA
Look, I'm not conducting a social experiment, I'm getting married to somebody I love.

CARRIE
But for the child. . .

SARA
We're talking about raising a family in love.

CARRIE
I don't want to take sides, Sara.

SARA
Really.

Rising, calling to Waitress:

Could I have the check?

CARRIE
I don't think it's racist to be discriminating.

Sara starts going out. Angrily:

You're the one walking out, Sara, not me!

Sara is gone, Carrie alone. She controls the impulse to cry, puts creamer in her coffee, stirs it. Bitterly:

That's not fair, Sara. That's really not fair.

She sips coffee. Fade.

Clubs

Actors portray the same characters at three stages of life. First, as small children. Two girls play in a sandbox. Boy approaches.

BEV
Ok, you make the castle and I'll make the wall. Pack it real hard.

DAN
Can I play?

BEV
No, this is for girls.

DAN
I can play too.

BEV
This is a club for girls. You gotta be in the club.

DAN
What club?

BEV
The Girls' Sandbox Club.

DAN
Wanta play dinosaurs?

BEV
Dinosaurs are all dead.

DAN
I can draw.

HONEY
No you can't.

DAN
I can draw a horse. In the sand. *(drawing)* I can draw good.

HONEY
Horses are dumb.

DAN
I wanta be in the club.

BEV
You like to play dolls?

DAN
No.

BEV
We're gonna play dolls.

DAN
Ok, I'll play.

HONEY *(calling out)*
Danny plays dolls! Danny's a sissy!

BEV
His sister said he pees in his bed.

DAN *(pointing to the sand)*
There's a horse.

BEV & HONEY
Peepee, peepee! Sissy pissy, sissy pissy!

DAN
I spilled some water!

BEV
His sister saw his tinky.

HONEY
Let's play guns. And shoot Danny!

BEV
Shoot off his tinky!

They swarm around him, shooting.

You're dead! You have to die!

He stands motionless, trying not to cry.

BEV
Danny's gonna cry! Danny's gonna cry!

HONEY
End of recess.

Bev stomps all over the drawing.

BEV *(going out)*
He messed up the game. You get shot you die. Dummy!

They go out, leaving him in misery. Freeze.

Each is given a new costume element. They animate, now as teenagers in a classroom after school.

HONEY
We're doing this new one.

She demonstrates a cheerleading routine to Dan. Bev comes in, is ignored.

DAN

Cool. Only do more stuff for the linemen. Jeez, I'm gonna make All-State. I should get a cheer whenever I knock somebody on his ass.

HONEY

It sounds funny to yell, "Wibberly, Wibberly!"

DAN

No, come on! "Dan the Man! Dan the Man!"

BEV

Excuse me. Is this where the yearbook committee is?

HONEY

Yes.

BEV

Mr. Miller said I was supposed to be the editor or something?

DAN

Hi.

BEV

I'm Beverly Shoemaker.

HONEY

I'm Honey.

DAN *(ignoring Bev)*

Dan Wibberly.

BEV

Oh, I know who both of you are. I'm very glad to—

HONEY

Let's get started.

BEV

Where's the other people on the. . .

HONEY

You're sposed to know that. You're sposed to be the editor.

BEV

Joellen was, but she quit. So, well, gee, I have sort of an agenda.

DAN

A what?

HONEY

Well we were going to break into committees, and Dan and I are the photo committee. So why don't you talk to the other people and do something with them, and Dan and I will go through these candids and write captions.

BEV
Ok, well, they're not here, so maybe I could help out. . . I wrote a list of things from previous years, maybe we could put these on different ones. . .

HONEY
Uh-huh.

DAN *(reading from her list)*
"A good sport."

HONEY
"Preparing for the future." That's very nice.

DAN
You got that one of Mary?

HONEY
Coming out of the locker room, with the towel? She'll die!

DAN
Here it is!

BEV
She's so pretty.

DAN
Huh?

BEV
Mary Turner is so pretty.

DAN
She's a cow. Ok, we gotta find a good caption.

BEV
How about. . . "Spring Morning?"

DAN
I got it: "Oh, was this supposed to be formal?"

HONEY
She'll die! There's Mark.

DAN
What's that?

HONEY
That's Karen's party. God, everybody's in that. *(aware of Bev)* I don't mean everybody, I mean everybody that's. . .

DAN *(looking at photo)*
What's that?

HONEY
That's the class play.

DAN
"Faggots on Parade."

Honey laughs.

No. *(lisping)* "My goodnesth! Mr. Miller is such a sthweetie!"

BEV *(pointing)*
Oh, that's me. I just had a little part. I always look funny when I take off my glasses.

DAN
Ok, so you can write a caption.

BEV
I couldn't write for my own picture.

HONEY
Tell you what. Why don't you get the other pictures, in Mr. Miller's room, and look for stuff that might fit one of these.

BEV
Oh. Ok.

She goes out. Dan takes the photo.

DAN
Lemme see that. "I didn't know I left my boobs at home."

Prints it on the list.

HONEY
Come on, she is a jerk but that's a bit—

DAN
I wanta puke. "I'm sposed to be the editor or something." How'd we get stuck with Miss Hemorrhoids?

HONEY
Mr. Miller.

DAN
Fags.

HONEY
We could just take off.

DAN
Look, after practice I'll get Cindy and Matt, and we'll come over to your place and do this.

HONEY
We can have some beer. My folks don't care.

DAN
All right! Bout eight?

HONEY

Bye.

Bev comes in, having heard them. She sees the list. Reads. Starts to erase it violently. Freeze.

Each is given a different costume element. They animate, now in a busy Manhattan coffee shop. Honey is waitress. Bev sits at a table.

BEV

Hi, could I have a—

HONEY *(as waitress)*

Hold on.

Dan enters, with shoulderbag, mildly gay mannerisms. Looks around for a seat.

DAN

Scuse me, is anybody sitting here? You mind?

Bev gestures assent.

Coffee and a plain doughnut, please.

HONEY

In a minute.

DAN

La-dee-dah.

BEV

Good luck.

DAN

God, I can spot 'em. Thirty years old, Profession Actress, "studied with Uta Hagen," never been cast. In this city, they are mass-produced.

BEV

Really.

HONEY *(returning)*

Can I get you something?

DAN

Coffee and a plain doughnut.

BEV

Maybe a menu?

HONEY *(rushing off after menu)*

Sorry.

BEV *(to Dan)*

Is my watch right?

DAN
Quarter of three.

BEV
I'm on a tight schedule. It's a little nerve-wracking.

DAN
Same here.

Honey brings menus.

BEV
Tell you, could I just have a plain salad, oil and vinegar, whole wheat toast, diet coke.

HONEY
Yeh. *(to Dan)* Sorry, did you want one slice or two?

DAN
You slice your doughnuts?

HONEY
Oh. Sorry. *(to Bev)* You look familiar.

DAN
You act familiar.

Honey starts to react, goes out.

BEV
Ouch.

DAN
I know. I'm sorry. I just get very . . . tacky sometimes with people who want to be part of the club. Actually, you do look familiar.

BEV
"If it's soft enough for baby's tender skin. . ."

DAN
Yes! The Charmin Girl! Omigod, a celebrity! Is it really that soft?

BEV
Well try it!

They laugh.

DAN
But that's fabulous. That's very good money.

BEV
Really. Although I don't want to spend my whole career in toilet paper.

HONEY *(returning)*
Did you say coffee?

DAN
Yes, and could I have real milk instead of the artificial?

HONEY
If you want to order milk.

DAN
Love you too, honey.

She stops. Tired rage:

HONEY
In fact, my name is Honey, thank you.

Goes out.

DAN *(indicating Honey)*
Well! Let's buy brains for our Barbie!

They laugh. He picks up a napkin, starts sketching.

BEV
Are you an artist?

DAN
Designer.

BEV
Of what?

DAN
Oh, this and that. Couple of bands, new club, some very upscale interiors. I've had some nice write-ups. I'm doing a fabulous new restaurant up on East 53rd.

Holds up napkin. Caricature of the waitress.

BEV
Oh, that is so cruel! God, now *she* looks familiar.

DAN
In this city, everybody looks familiar. It's because we all feel we've escaped from our old home town, and the posse is tracking us down.

BEV
Did you ever think, if you ran into somebody from high school—

DAN
Ohhhhh God!

BEV
Me with glasses, bad breath—

DAN
Macho man, that was me. Football, All-State tackle, totally brain-dead.

BEV
Gaaaa! I was terrified of the athletes, cheerleaders—

DAN
I was terrified. I come from a fairly small town, Newark, Delaware—

BEV
No no no.

DAN
Yes yes yes. You know it? It's a godawful little hole. My name's Daniel, in high school they called me Dan the Man. And I was so terrified somebody would pull off my helmet and say "Ah-hah! Here's one! Sissy!"

He laughs. After a moment:

BEV
Who was your high school valedictorian?

DAN
God, Beverly something. . .

BEV
Describe her.

DAN
Oh, I don't know. Something the Roto-Rooter coughed up.

BEV
Well I wouldn't go that far.

Silence. He realizes, gasps, nearly collapses, then bursts out:

DAN
Oh may God strike me dead! Ahhhhhhhhhhhhhh! No! Yes! I can't believe it! You look so totally different! Oh God! God, I didn't mean—

BEV
I know—

DAN
But you look so totally— What *happened?*

BEV
It's a very long story.

Ad lib. Laughter.

DAN
Well, how *are* you?

BEV
Really fine. Yeh, I really am. I've got a great agency: Marie Lecompte.

DAN
Oh God, they do marvelous things with girls. Oh! I've got so many things to tell you!

BEV
You've changed.

DAN
Well— Yes. Yes, just a bit. *(laughing)* Well you know, I got to college, and I totally fell apart. My grades were down to here, they kicked me off the team—

So I took this art class thinking it was going to be a piece of cake. And it was the hardest thing I'd ever done in my life, and I loved it.

BEV
So you're happy.

DAN
God, I love it. Finally, I belong. I really belong. And there must be some kind of worm in the apple, I mean, because I do have this little mean streak about four lanes wide. But I have to admit, yes, I'm happy. *(looking around)* Where is our food?!

BEV
It's a shame so many people do work they don't care about.

DAN
Oh, this is so great! Listen, I'm doing this show, it's terrific, it's like leather leather leather, only I want to get away from models that look like the Mafia in drag. I want some real—

BEV
Girl-next-door. That's me. I'd love it. A degenerate Girl Scout.

Laughter.

Or how about leather toilet paper?

They are in hysterics. Honey returns.

HONEY
Anything else?

A hitch: she hasn't served anything. They continue laughing.

DAN

No. That's fine.

BEV

You said your name was Honey?

HONEY

Yeh.

She leaves the check. They break up again. They get up, get ready to go.

BEV

I knew a Honey. I used to cry myself to sleep at night wishing I could be like her.

DAN

God. . .

BEV

But whenever I'm supposed to do a shoot where I need to be really, really full of life, I think of her.

DAN

Listen, give me a call. There's a great party this weekend, You'll meet a lot of people. I've got a million things to tell you. And we can talk over old times.

BEV

New times.

DAN

New times.

They go out. Honey cleans up table, picks up the napkin, looks at it. Blackout.

What's Buried

Living room of an empty house. Trish, a woman about forty, enters, looking around.

OLLIE *(off)*
You down here?

TRISH
Living room.

Ollie, her husband, appears, followed by Mr. & Mrs. Byers, an older African-American couple.

OLLIE
Couldn't find you.

TRISH
I was just checking what we left in the kitchen. Well, so you saw everything.

MR. BYERS
Great house.

MRS. BYERS
It is just beautiful.

MR. BYERS
Nice bedrooms.

TRISH
Did you see everything?

MRS. BYERS
We did.

OLLIE
The grand tour.

TRISH
It's been a good old house for us. One thing I really love is the space. We walked in here the first time, and look clear on in through to the kitchen, wow. And the dining-room mirrors—

MRS. BYERS
I like the mirrors.

OLLIE
That's what our kids are gonna miss. Eleven and six, and they still make faces in the mirror.

MRS. BYERS
Oh I just worry about— *(laughing)* We be eating dinner and Dwight won't ever look at me none, cause he'll be seeing his own self in the mirror!

MR. BYERS *(laughing)*
I'll look at you, woman. Don't think I won't!

TRISH
And this is all the original woodwork. They did a little piecing on the floor here, but otherwise. . .

MR. BYERS
Why are you moving?

OLLIE
Well, it's a bunch of things—

TRISH
Richard's going into middle school, and Sara's just starting, and—

OLLIE
And I grew up in the country, I like a little more green around—

TRISH
Although there is a back yard here—

MR. BYERS
You been on the market a while?

OLLIE
Well that's why we're showing it ourselves. The realtor we had didn't really do much. So we figured. . .

TRISH
No, we really enjoyed it here, but. . .

OLLIE
When I first brought it up, Trish just looked at me and said—

Flashback. Mr. & Mrs. Byers freeze. Ollie and Trish are in the middle of an argument.

TRISH
Move?

OLLIE
Well I'm just bringing it up.

TRISH
I love it here. What about Richard? Sara?

OLLIE
Don't jump all over me!

TRISH

Why?

OLLIE

I talked to two realtors. We're going to have a very difficult time getting our money out of this place. Property here is taking a nosedive.

TRISH

Why?

OLLIE

Take a look.

TRISH

At what?

OLLIE

At the neighborhood. People moving in. . .

TRISH

So?

OLLIE

It's not safe.

TRISH

Safe? I feel safe.

OLLIE

I don't mean it's not safe. But it's the perception. There's three houses on the block that are still single-family. Everything else is apartments. That's a different class of people—

TRISH

A different class—

OLLIE

I don't mean a worse class. I mean a different class—

TRISH

Ollie—

Back to the present.

Ollie, did you turn off the lights upstairs?

OLLIE

Yep.

MRS. BYERS

I should look at the kitchen again—

TRISH

Sure.

MRS. BYERS

Is there a way to get gas hooked up here? I don't like to cook on electric.

TRISH

Right back there.

Trish indicates the kitchen, walks her to the door. Mrs. Byers goes out.

OLLIE

So are you folks from around here?

MR. BYERS

Yeh. We've been at Fifth and Lemon, for, oh, nineteen years, but our daughter's moving back in with us, with our grandson, and that's one of those things looks like it's gonna be for a while. And that area's not very safe now—

OLLIE

Well that's one thing around here, it's safe—

MR. BYERS

And her little boy, Michael, he'll be starting to school, so we're kinda worried about that—

OLLIE

Well you saw the school, it's just two blocks, Sara woulda been going there, it's a nice mix of kids—

Flashback. Byers freezes. Ollie and Trish quarrel.

Sixty percent minority. I mean that's not a problem in itself, it's an advantage in some ways—

TRISH

Ollie—

OLLIE

But you know what's happening, place like that, they cut the budget, the good teachers get out, you get ten-year-old kids with knives. It's a fact.

TRISH

I don't know. . . It's so close, and then I think of her walking by that intersection with those . . . people that hang out there. . .

OLLIE

It'd be nice to have a yard, big yard they could play in.

Back to the present. Mrs. Byers returns.

MRS. BYERS

I love the backyard. We just got an alley running out back.

TRISH
It's little, but it's nice for flowers.

MRS. BYERS
My grandma had geraniums, so Michael's grandma is gonna plant geraniums!

OLLIE
Don't have to mow it or anything.

MR. BYERS *(laughing)*
That's good by me.

TRISH
Richard and his friends, they were always out there. They made a little cubby-hole under the porch. And the pets—

OLLIE
Couple pets had funerals there.

TRISH
Star. Remember Star?

Flashback. Ollie and Trish speak as if to child.

Oh Star. . . Richard, honey, you awake? Honey, poor Star died last night. We thought she would.

OLLIE
She's quiet now.

TRISH
But we'll bury her in the back yard, ok? And we can make a gravestone, and she'll always be there.

OLLIE
We'll always have our Star.

Back to the present.

Star. . . Yeh. Cat.

MRS. BYERS
Cat. We've got three cats.

MR. BYERS
Three cats have got *us.*

TRISH
Well, anyway, so. . .

OLLIE
So, think about it and give us a call—

MRS. BYERS
We will. Oh, and the woodwork!

MR. BYERS
It's a great house.

OLLIE
It is. I hate to leave it. I really hate it.

Flashback. Trish and Ollie.

I hate it. I hate *them.*

TRISH
What?

OLLIE
People coming through here, looking at the house. It's our damn house. Oh they're nice people, they're fine, I hope they buy it. But I just—

The thought of being replaced, bumped out. This is our roots. We've got things buried here. We made two babies, and we had ten dozen quarrels, and we made up ten dozen times, and your mother fell down the stairs, and the cat peed on the carpet and—

I love this place.

TRISH
I love it—

OLLIE
I love it. So why are we moving?

TRISH
We're moving because we are being moved. The neighborhood, ok, but the neighborhood was the Collinses, who moved away. Old lady, Mrs. Dickerson, on the corner, she's gone. The tree in the alley, they took that out.

OLLIE
I'm very confused right now.

TRISH
It's nothing personal, Ollie. It's my choice too. It's a matter of dollars and cents. And the kids.

OLLIE
I'm very confused.

Back to the present.

TRISH
What's the matter?

OLLIE
Nothing. I was kinda confused. Trying to remember—

TRISH
It's funny to see it empty.

MR. BYERS
I know that feeling.

MRS. BYERS
It sure is.

OLLIE
Well so, any questions, or—?

MR. BYERS
No. We'll talk it over, give you a call right away.

OLLIE
I think you'd get some good value here.

MRS. BYERS
I love it. I really do.

TRISH
There's a lot buried there.

OLLIE
Goodbye, Star. You get the lights?

TRISH
Sure.

Ollie starts walking out with Mr. & Mrs. Byers. Trish stands, waiting to turn off the lights.

OLLIE
You have just the one daughter?

MRS. BYERS
No, we've got three. Two girls and a boy. Two grandkids. Three cats.

OLLIE
Cats.

They are out. Trish, alone:

TRISH
Goodbye, Star.

Blackout.

CONFESSION

A narrow table. At one end, Raymond sits in a wooden chair. He is about forty, in suit and white shirt without a tie, somewhat rumpled. He speaks slowly, objectively, with no emotion.

At the opposite end, a Police Stenographer, focused on her work, writing as the others are speaking. The Detective goes through a familiar routine.

Long pause. Detective shifts weight.

RAYMOND
I can't say unless you ask me something.

DETECTIVE
Then what did you do?

RAYMOND
Ok, when we were about to get in the car, I saw another car coming, which I thought looked like it might be stopping, but it didn't. And so we stood there, and when that car had gone I told him to get in the car. And he did and he didn't struggle.
And I started driving off. And he started crying and down toward 48th I thought about letting him go.

DETECTIVE
But you didn't?

RAYMOND
No.

DETECTIVE
You didn't.

RAYMOND
No.

DETECTIVE
Then what did you do?

RAYMOND
Ok. I ran a red light, and then up a dirt road, over some railroad tracks, turned left over and parked the car over the side of the railroad tracks, and I told him get out of the car.

DETECTIVE
The Ford Pinto?

Pause.

RAYMOND
There was snow on the ground.

STENO
Excuse me. Did he say the Ford Pinto?

DETECTIVE
I said the Ford Pinto. He didn't respond.

RAYMOND
It was the Ford Pinto, yes sir.

STENO
Sorry. I'm new at this.

RAYMOND
That's ok.

Pause.

There was snow on the ground. We turned into the woods. I told him stop here, if he did what I told him to, nothing would happen. I told him take off his clothes. Which he did.

Then I told him to lay on his back. He didn't want to. So I placed my hands on his shoulders, and indicated with some pressure that he should lay back, but not squeezing.

DETECTIVE
Not squeezing?

RAYMOND
Not squeezing at that time.

Pause.

DETECTIVE
Then what did you do?

RAYMOND
Ok, when he had done that, with his back to the ground, not directly on the ground, but on some leaves on the ground in the snow, then this must have been about two o'clock. Because I looked at my watch and I remembered I'd missed lunch.

But it was funny because I hadn't, I'd had a BLT and some coffee. And then I knelt on his chest and started to strangle him.

DETECTIVE
Knelt on his chest?

RAYMOND
With my knees.

DETECTIVE
And his back on the ground?

RAYMOND
In the snow.

Pause.

Could I take a minute?

DETECTIVE
You need the bathroom?

RAYMOND
No.

DETECTIVE *(to Stenographer)*
Indicate the time.

Pause.

Is Larry done? Can he come in and witness?

STENO
He said he'd come in as soon as he could.

DETECTIVE
I don't wanta do this over.

STENO
I don't know. Can't he witness when he signs it?

DETECTIVE
Could you stop with the gum? I got a thing about that.

STENO
Sorry.

RAYMOND
Ok. I'm ok.

Pause.

I can't say unless you ask me something.

DETECTIVE
Ok. Then what did you do?

RAYMOND
He struggled and seemed to be in pain, so I stabbed him a couple of times, just not very much, and he just looked rather uncertain. And I just wasn't sure what to do. And he asked me then to go to the hospital, because he was in pain, and I stabbed him a great many times.

DETECTIVE
Why?

RAYMOND
Just to be sure he was dead.

Pause.

I'm having some trouble here right now.

DETECTIVE
Take your time.

Raymond remains setting, shifting position several times. Stenographer sits absolutely frozen. Detective walks around the table, then sits again on the table edge. To Stenographer:

You doing ok? Enjoying your work?

RAYMOND
Ok. I'm ok.

Pause.

I can't say unless you ask me something.

DETECTIVE
Did you plan to do this?

RAYMOND
I don't think so. No.

DETECTIVE
You're saying there was no pre-planning involved?

RAYMOND
Not to my knowledge.

DETECTIVE
What did you plan to do?

RAYMOND
I don't know.

DETECTIVE
Why did you do it?

RAYMOND
No reason I can think of. I'm sure there was some reason.

DETECTIVE
Did you at any time fondle, touch privately, play with, do anything personal with this boy?

RAYMOND
Nothing at all.

DETECTIVE
No sexual advances whatsoever of any kind?

RAYMOND
None at all.

DETECTIVE
Were you planning to make some form of sexual advances to this boy?

RAYMOND
No. Not at all.

DETECTIVE
Have you been at any time ever sexually involved with any males?

RAYMOND
Never.

DETECTIVE
Have you been at any time ever sexually involved with any females?

RAYMOND
Never.

DETECTIVE
Not ever.

RAYMOND
Never.

DETECTIVE
Have you been at any time ever sexually active in any way?

RAYMOND
No.

Pause.

Should I talk some more about that, or whatever?

DETECTIVE
I think that's about it for now.

Vaguely, more or less to Stenographer.

These pathetic sonsabitches. At Comstock they took one of these guys, they shoved a coke bottle up his ass, and then they broke it. Don't ask me how.

STENO
Did you want that in the transcript?

DETECTIVE
Sorry. No offence intended.

Looks at her pad, then to Raymond.

Ok honey buns, let's go out and you can wait. We'll get this witnessed, and then we can leave you to play with yourself.

Raymond gets up, waits. Detective goes to the door, followed by Raymond, then halts. Raymond halts. Detective speaks in a flat tone:

You know something? I'm talking to you, twinkie-pie. I've got a fifteen year old son. You don't know how lucky you are. You just don't know how fucking . . . fucking lucky you are.

RAYMOND

I'm sorry.

DETECTIVE

Don't push it.

Meanwhile, the Stenographer has gathered her supplies, walked to door, waiting. Detective starts to open door, looks back. Raymond follows.

As he passes, the Stenographer moans, grabs him, strikes at him with her pencil, claws at his face, out of control, with frantic, suppressed moans of rage. Raymond covers his face limply.

The Detective, after a moment's surprise, intervenes, struggles to bring her under control.

Sally! Stop it! Stop it for Chrissake! *(to Raymond)* You stand right there, don't move a fucking inch! *(to Stenographer)* Straighten out! Stop! I'm telling you stop! Stop! Stop!

He holds her. At last she gives up, exhausted. He supports her over to sit in Raymond's chair. Raymond stands at a distance. Long silence, except for her sobbing.

Oh Christ. What the hell. What a terrific day.

STENO

I'm sorry. . .

DETECTIVE

Anybody give you the information that we have rules, we have procedural rules?

STENO

I just. . .

DETECTIVE

You just shit in your own shoe. I have to report this.

STENO
Doug. . .

DETECTIVE
I have to report this. Now don't give me any shit. *(to Raymond)* You have any abrasions?

Raymond removes his hand. His right cheek has a deep gash, bleeding.

Oh Christ. *(to Stenographer)* What the hell do you think you're doing? You know how long it's gonna take till the chief takes a chance on hiring another woman? Oh Christ.

STENO
Doug. . . I really need this job. I was just too. . .

DETECTIVE
"Oh Doug, I just don't know what came over me!"

STENO
It won't happen—

DETECTIVE
It sure as hell won't. You're out on your ass.

STENO
Doug, I went to night school for three years—

DETECTIVE
I don't want to hear it—

STENO
I never got a cent of child support, I went through two wage cuts and three lay-offs, and I'd see my little baby's face up to the window watching me go—

DETECTIVE
I don't wanta hear it—

STENO
Doug!

DETECTIVE
Gimme all the excuses. And your husband's a drunk, and he beat you up, and this and that, and your personal needs, and the violence of society, and blah blah blah. Surprise me. You're just pathetic.

STENO
Doug, I really need this job.

RAYMOND
Excuse me. . .

They look at him. Long pause.

It's all right with me. I don't want her to get in trouble. It's no problem. I'd prefer it if we could just not. . . Could we just finish the. . .

DETECTIVE *(ignoring him)*
Sally, I'm sorry. It's not an option. They take a look at him, "What happened?" "Oh, he had an itch. And scratched it." And then his lawyer gets on it, and very soon we're testifying under oath, and Sally, I need my job too.

Pause.

This job is garbage collecting. You pick it up, cart it off the sidewalk. You don't go crazy and stomp around on the leftovers. That's what they do at the dump. This is a job. We have rules for stuff that leaves marks.

Opens door.

Ron, can you come in here a minute?

Silence. Sally looks up at Raymond.

RAYMOND
We have some aspects in common.

STENO
Jesus Christ. . .

She tries to speak, fails. Fade.

Party Time

Note: this piece was first staged in multiple areas, lights up and down on each scene. A later staging put the old couple on two tall stepladders, above the action, with each scenic group coming around to the front of the stepladder, changing the configuration of chairs in the same center area. Either works.

An old couple watches TV.

OLD WOMAN *(to us)*
Hello there. This is God.

OLD MAN
It is.

OLD WOMAN
People ask me and my husband, they say "What is God doing in a two-room walk-up on 48th and Market?" But you know, fixed income, and they're cutting Medicare. Plus, we don't like the suburbs.

Old Man clicks remote. Sound of TV.

Would you turn that off?

OLD MAN
Some kinda silly stuff.

OLD WOMAN
We feel more in touch here. If he'd stop watching that TV.

OLD MAN
Somebody's poor excuse for life.

OLD WOMAN
What you got on there?

OLD MAN
Have you been fooling with this? That looks like those young people downstairs.

OLD WOMAN
I switched the cable.

OLD MAN
What you doing that for?

OLD WOMAN
Because I'm God.

OLD MAN
Fix it back there. I want to see that show where they talk about dirty stuff.

OLD WOMAN
You are the limit.

OLD MAN
It's you that's spying on the neighbors.

OLD WOMAN
"Her eye is on the sparrow."

OLD MAN
And a lot more than that.

They chuckle.

I remember when we could sit on the front stoop. People passing by.

OLD WOMAN
Well who's on there then?

OLD MAN
It's those kids downstairs.

OLD WOMAN
I can't hear'em.

OLD MAN
It's better that way.

OLD WOMAN
Tune that in.

OLD MAN
How do you do this *(punching at it)* damn thing?

OLD WOMAN
Just poke it and pray.

They sit and watch. Lights. An apartment in the building. Jeff is cleaning up.

JEFF
Why not call people, tell'em not to come?

JOHN
Jeff, look, here's my idea. First, forget the people in the building, they're just assholes. Second, we can try to keep it down, ok?

JEFF
That's your idea? Look, we're gonna have twenty, thirty people, six cases of beer—

JOHN
Pretzels.

JEFF
And we've got the neighbors on us, the landlord, the cops— John, the bloom is off.

JOHN
The landlord's cool: nobody can find him. And the cops are more pissed at the neighbors: it's not us keeps calling'em.

JEFF
Maybe I just don't like to—

JOHN
Look, seriously, hey I'm kidding, ok? We'll try to keep it a little more under control, ok?

JEFF
People like Larry— They're maniacs.

JOHN
Oh come on.

JEFF
Yeh, by day they're bank tellers and management trainees and waiters and law students. By night they're maniacs. Look, John, I didn't know this was going to become Party Central—

JOHN
Says he. Hey, what is it, now that you're tight with Jenny, now you'll just have your own party, is that it?

Jeff makes a frustrated, futile gesture, gives up. Jen enters with a grocery sack.

JEN
Party time!

Hugs Jeff, goes toward kitchen with sack.

JOHN
Talk to this guy, would you? He's in a sweat about the neighbors.

JEFF
I didn't plan for this party. I don't want this party. I'm tired.

JEN
Ok, so sleep. This is for Donna's birthday. She's my friend.

JEFF
I had two neighbors talk to me today—

JEN
They have been bitching ever since we moved in. Ever since

they saw Bob come in here. They don't like it that some of our friends are not lily-white. Bob and Christine, they don't like the color combination—

JEFF

I don't see that.

JEN

And they have done everything they could— They told the police we were a whorehouse because they saw men come in here, and clearly Bob must be my pimp, so don't give me this crap about the neighbors—

JEFF

Jen—

JEN

Those old farts upstairs have their TV up full blast, does anybody complain about them?

Reaction from above:

OLD MAN

Was that us?

OLD WOMAN

I heard that!

JEFF

I just—

JEN

Ok, I'll warn them. So they know we're gonna start. They can't get upset. Fair warning. *(banging chair on floor)* Party time!

Light change. The old couple watches TV.

OLD WOMAN

That's gonna get violent.

OLD MAN

I don't know what we're seein here.

OLD WOMAN

Real life.

OLD MAN

I'm gettin up.

OLD WOMAN

You ain't walkin good.

OLD MAN

I'm gettin up!

OLD WOMAN
Don't get salty.

OLD MAN
I'm sittin down.

OLD WOMAN
You old bird.

OLD MAN
Change the channel.

Points selector, changes channel. Lights. Shift. Dave and Clarice at dinner table.

DAVE
Hear that? Going on up there?

CLARICE
It's awful.

DAVE
Awful. You call that awful? That's nothing.

CLARICE
Did you talk to them?

DAVE
It's past the talking stage.

CLARICE
How we got stuck here—

DAVE
Tell me about it. Right, I asked for a long-term lease. I got it.

CLARICE
Want another beer?

DAVE
They're free to come and go. I'm sick of it. Same thing all day. These people sitting on the street, shove their can in my face. Get your can outa my face. I want somebody to call doing a survey, cause I got a lot of opinions.

CLARICE
It's bad.

DAVE
Same stuff at work. In your face. Everything in your face. People in and out of there day and night, all kinds of people, black guy with a white girl— what're they doing there?

CLARICE
What?

DAVE
Figure it out.

CLARICE
Maybe friends.

DAVE
Friends.

CLARICE
Dave—

DAVE
"Dave." What? Dave Dave Dave. What?

CLARICE
Don't yell at me.

DAVE
That's not yelling. You want yelling, come to my office.

CLARICE
I think if you call the police again you shouldn't say anything about a black man like you did before, because then they think it's not about the noise, they just think you're—

DAVE
Think I'm what?

Silence. Shouts:

Think I'm what?!!!

No response.

I need some scotch.

Lights. The old couple watch TV.

OLD WOMAN
Why don't they have happy stuff?

OLD MAN
You wanted real life, you got it.

Myron is studying, reading a large volume and taking notes. Kim enters, bringing him a cup of coffee.

KIM
Where's the yelling?

MYRON
205. And 302. She want anything?

KIM
She's not awake.

MYRON

Listen to this:

Whoever comes to shroud me, do not harm
Nor question much
That subtle wreath of hair which crowns my arm—

KIM

Don't read me that stuff. I can't understand it.

MYRON

He's talking about—

KIM

It's depressing.

MYRON

I went up there twice. "My mother's sick, could you keep it down?" They look at you like, "What, you got a problem?"

KIM

She doesn't hear it.

MYRON

I do. You do. At least in the hospital it was quiet there. You could go there, sleep a few hours. She's gonna get better, she was talking a little bit today.

KIM

No she's not. She's home to die. You know that.

MYRON

How's school?

KIM

Ok.

MYRON

You going to classes?

KIM

Yeh I'm going. I skipped two classes but they know Mom's sick.

MYRON

Will you stop missing classes? I'm staying here so you wouldn't miss classes. I've got my damn comprehensives next month, and I'm here taking care of Mom and taking care of you when I can't even take care of myself—

KIM

Want something to eat?

MYRON

Not your cooking. Who taught you to make coffee? This sucks.

KIM

Well aren't we full of sunshine! Look, Myron, she can't hear. Maybe the vibrations keep her heart going. And you're sleeping at Jerry's, you're getting sleep, she's getting sleep, I'm not complaining—

MYRON

It's the principle of the thing. They treat you like you don't exist. You're a minor inconvenience. You're a dog turd. Hell, I already feel like that. What am I gonna do with a master's in English Lit?

KIM

Write a book or something.

MYRON

For the first time I understand the concept of Hamlet as crazed serial killer.

KIM

Myron—

MYRON

They've got their own little world up there, and nothing else exists. You don't exist, she don't exist—

KIM

Doesn't.

MYRON

Shut up with that! I'm the college graduate!

KIM

Then act like it.

MYRON *(shouting at ceiling)*

Ahhh— Shut! Up!

Lights. Shift. Old couple:

OLD WOMAN

All this crazy stuff. Should we move to the suburbs?

OLD MAN

If I woke up in the morning, how would I know I wasn't dead?

OLD WOMAN

See what's on the Christian channel.

OLD MAN

All that God stuff.

OLD WOMAN

Well it's quiet.

He punches remote. Lights. Shift. A couple in bed, he reading the Bible, she staring at the ceiling.

ANN

Richard, could you turn the light off pretty soon?

RICHARD

Almost finished.

ANN

You're up early tomorrow.

Silence.

I can't believe you're lying there reading that.

RICHARD

What?

ANN

Reading the Word of God, while this is going on above us.

RICHARD

I can concentrate.

ANN

You don't know what that does to me.

RICHARD

Well I pray for them.

ANN

To lie here and listen to that. Do you think I don't know, you think I'm that sheltered, that I don't know exactly what's going on above our heads, because I know.

RICHARD

Ann, I talked to them, I gave them three pamphlets. They're not ready to receive. Look, I have to be up at 6:30—

ANN

Well you're the one that wants to be a minister. I'm your partner in this, but it's not my idea, and if you're going to dedicate yourself then why not start now, if that's where the souls need saving—

RICHARD

I'm not a minister yet. I work at the post office. We don't save souls at the post office.

Ann, I feel for these people. These people are lost, they're isolated, it's as if the whole world was crammed into this apartment building, and we're all shut off in our little rooms, shut away from the light.

And they feel as if all their joy and their celebration has to be crammed into this one evening, they have to throw themselves at it like jumping in front of a truck—

ANN

Well that's fascinating.

RICHARD

I think we need to worry less about what's going on up there but maybe more what's going on down here.

ANN

Well— What do you mean, "What's going on down here?"

RICHARD

Ann, I love you.

ANN

Yes.

RICHARD

Yes? That's it?

ANN

I said I love you.

RICHARD

Saying and showing are two different things. I want to be a pastor, not a priest.

ANN

Well you're the one staying up reading.

RICHARD

Because I don't know how to reach out to you—

ANN

Well, all this party thing I think puts a strain on our relationship.

RICHARD

You're blaming our lack of intimacy on a party?

ANN

On constant partying above our bedroom. This is not easy for me, Richard, I have very strong feelings. . . But it's a question of . . . concentration.

RICHARD

Darling, we're alone here. This is our consecrated bed. There is only you and me. You and me.

He embraces her gently. A sudden burst of whooping and cheers. Lights. Old couple.

OLD WOMAN
They always sneak that dirty stuff in.

OLD MAN
Never trust those preachers.

He punches remote. Lights. Jeff is in the bedroom, brooding. John enters.

JOHN
Why you in the bedroom?

JEFF
Partying.

JOHN
What about you invite all the neighbors? At least we'd offer.

Jeff glares at John. Jen comes in, drunk, hugs Jeff.

JEN
What's up?

JEFF
I didn't plan for this party. I didn't want this party. It's only nine o'clock and it's already out of control—

JEN
Party pooper.

JEFF
John, ok, I moved in, bachelor pad, fantastic. And just the freedom and friends and people around—

JEN
Fantastic—

JEFF
Ok, and people, all kinds of people, bring people together, this is where it's happening, this is where I belong.

JEN
Bring us together—

JEFF
And Christ, we're all in our little cubicles, compartments, driving us nuts, we need, somewhere, anywhere, just one big, beautiful party. It was beautiful, John. . .

JEN
Wheeee!

JEFF
And then this. Blast. Bellow. Booze. Puke. And you hanging off everybody's neck to show what a free spirit you are.

JEN *(walking out)*
Oh I don't need this!

JOHN
Hey, ok, it was loud. But now it's mellowing out.

Huge roar. Lights. Old couple.

OLD WOMAN
I don't know how much more of that I can stand.

OLD MAN
Just don't take it out on me.

He punches remote. Lights. Kim and Myron. He slams his book shut, paces.

KIM
Myron, would you just do something? You don't need to stay here. Come back in the morning when I have to go to class. You're driving me crazy.

MYRON
I'm getting out of here!

KIM
Then go!

MYRON
I can't! It's the principle of the thing. They have no right to intrude their existence on me.

KIM
How bout I call for a pizza?

MYRON
What's that supposed to accomplish?

KIM
It accomplishes dinner. Don't they teach you that in grad school?

MYRON
If I go up there I'm gonna lose it.

KIM
Put my Walkman on.

MYRON
So I lock myself into my head? Why don't I just crawl into the fridge and slam the door?

KIM
You just do that! Myron, I'm sick of this! You're my big brother, so act like it! You're acting like a five-year-old that didn't get invited to the party.

MYRON

You got it. Hey, it's not just 205, it's all over the country, they're throwing this party, it's party time, but I am not invited.

They got the beer, they got the chips, they got the balloons, they got the music going, the dancing, and I didn't get invited.

They got caviar and champagne, they got celebrities, and superstars, and geniuses, they got money coming out their nostrils.

And the jocks going "Myron writes poetry!" And the eggheads, "Oh he doesn't talk like us! He doesn't say *doesn't*!" Sure, let's party!

Pause.

That's it. I admit it. I don't want to go to any silly fucking party. But I want to be invited.

Lights. Party roar. Back to couple at dinner table. He has been drinking.

DAVE

What are you staring at me for?

CLARICE

I'm not staring.

DAVE

Saying it's my fault.

CLARICE

I'm not.

DAVE

Did I steal my own car?

CLARICE

What?

DAVE

When they stole the car? Stole it and set it on fire? It had to be those damn blacks, cause why else would they set it on fire?

CLARICE

Dave, those people up there are white!

DAVE

Then why are they making that noise?!!!

CLARICE

I'll go up there—

DAVE

What, you got something going on up there?

CLARICE
What?!—

He grabs her. Twists her arm.

Dave!

DAVE
Stop calling me Dave!

He releases her. Falls into his chair.

I'm sorry.

No response. Shouts:

I'm sorry! I'm sorry!! I'M SORRY!!!

Lights. Back to couple in bed.

ANN
Richard, I want to move, so we can live someplace nice, someplace quiet.

RICHARD
We can't afford it.

ANN
I want to work, so we can move.

RICHARD
Ann—

ANN
I want to work, but I'm not allowed to work.

RICHARD
I don't think it's right. Just for the sake of money.

ANN
Well for the sake of walls. And it might be nice if our car started, I would really like that.

RICHARD
The man works for the woman.

ANN
And the woman services the man.

RICHARD
It's not called service, it's called love. Ann, I— Let's pray then go to sleep. Ok? All right?

He goes to his knees. Suddenly she grabs a pillow and starts beating him.

Lights. Party roars. In the bedroom, Jen and John are embracing. Jeff enters.

JOHN

Oh hi.

Jeff makes a pointless gesture. Turns to go.

Hey, don't get mad. We were just talking.

JEN

Talking bout our fun-loving, partying roommate.

JEFF

Want me to party, I'll party. . .

Very drunk, he shoves John: no strength.

JOHN

Jeff, I'm sorry—

JEN

This is really stupid—

JEFF

I'll party. . .

JEN

You guys! We're friends! We're all friends! We're friends!!!

Party noise. All groups animate, in violent rage. Old couple rises with great difficulty, face their TV set, shouting at it to shut up.

OLD WOMAN & MAN

You there! Be quiet there! Sound like a herd of buffalo. Quiet down! That rickety racket you're makin! Not gonna take it!

Old Woman takes the channel select from him, points it at the set. Sudden cut-off. The characters are frozen in strife. Pause. Old Woman speaks to the TV, as if to a child.

OLD WOMAN

Now listen up. If God and her husband was living upstairs from you. And all the noise, and suffering, and strife, and wars and rumours of wars, and Hate Thy Neighbor As Thyself—

You know what she would do? She would just flip off this silly stuff, and take her pills, and go to bed with her husband.

Lights fade on the others.

OLD MAN

Help me get my back up.

OLD WOMAN

I hate when they talk about love. They don't know what love is. We knew what it was when we had some.

OLD MAN
I still got a little in me.

OLD WOMAN
Little bit. It perkles out every once in a while.

OLD MAN
Bout time for bed.

OLD WOMAN
Well come on here if you got some love.

They giggle, nuzzle, embrace. Fade.

Family Snapshots

Notes

Since 1969, we have written and produced hundreds of short sketches, micro-plays, ten-minute plays — whatever you call them. In 1979, some of our best work came together under the title *Families.* It's a subject people care about, and practically any play fits, by some stretch of the imagination, within that theme. In seven years, *Families* played over 200 performances throughout the country, for every sort of audience. Many of those sketches are included in our book *Rash Acts.*

In 1994, we returned to the "family" theme for a radio drama series, taking on a strange dramaturgical challenge: creating a series of 65 dramas, each complete in itself, 90 seconds in duration. *Family Snapshots* was carried on more than 80 stations, and we decided to create a stage version for touring, combining short pieces from this series with longer sketches.

Other challenges. Two minutes of air time feels much longer than two minutes of stage time. For the radio series, we'd used 26 actors, including kids, while on stage we were only a duo. On the radio, each piece began with realistic dialogue, made a sudden turn into inner monolog or vocal collage, then back to reality. On stage, making this clear without sound or lighting effects required much experiment with focus.

The experiment proved worthwhile. *Family Snapshots* has played in high schools, senior centers, libraries, universities, churches, rural arts series, and even in theatres. It's a mirror to which people bring their own images.

Producing the Show

Most of the notes prefacing *Dividing Lines* are relevant to *Family Snapshots.* Obviously, more sketches are included here than would fit in a show, and pieces from our book *Rash Acts* — particularly *Anniversary*, *Dalmatian*, *Doors*, *Bon Voyage*, and *Peace Negotiations* — can also be considered for inclusion.

The show can be of any length, though it's difficult to sustain more than an hour: a collection of short pieces is a very rich diet, fuller than the same stage time of a conventional play. We find that a good rhythm is to alternate a longer piece with two or three short pieces in succession, then another longer piece, etc.

All pieces in this collection can be performed with a maximum of three actors, and most of them with two. Or it's possible to do it as a large-cast show. In that case, several areas of the stage can be set, for a faster shift from one sketch to the next.

Be careful, though, to allow breathing space in the show. The audience needs time to absorb what they've experienced. We may use a musical bridge, a scene shift, or a span of talking informally with the audience — depending on the circumstance — to allow people to get back to equilibrium and have a moment with their own thoughts.

For many actors, the most difficult challenge in playing this material is to trust that an audience can actually ride the extreme swings between farcical and realistic, comic and tragic, frivolous and grim. Most plays have contrasts, of course, but within fairly tight tonal parameters. But shows like *Family Snapshots* or *Dividing Lines* work only if each piece is given its full value. The outlandish exaggeration of *Hot Fudge*, the quiet realism of *Coffee Shop*, the iconographic minimalism of *Chicken House*, and the rapid-fire collage of *Love* can work in the same show if it's clear that these styles are simply the most appropriate means to render this particular human experience. Above all, the show is *a telling of stories* that have their roots in reality.

How to convey this? In rehearsal, the cast must always come back to talking about what's *real* in the scenes: what's the real-life behavior this scene is referencing? We've seen student casts who have so much energy that the simple joy of performing carries a strong communicative intention. In our own performance, the audience is always aware that they're seeing a single couple performing everything, so our intention as story-tellers is in the foreground.

Finding a staging structure that suggests a story-telling mode can be helpful. For example, actors who aren't in the scene might be seated forward on the sides, watching the scene that's being played, then preparing and entering in full view of the audience. What's important is a sense of *stories being told.*

FAMILY

Bare stage. Three actors, one man and two women, come into positions facing upstage. Suddenly, all turn, erupt into center, playing as kids at recess.

ONE
Let's play house.

TWO
I don't want to play house, I want to play Star Wars.

THREE
Hey, Fantastic Four!

ONE
Ok, Fantastic Four in a house. I'll be the Mommy.

THREE
That's not Fantastic Four.

ONE
This is Fantastic Four playing house. I'll be the Mommy.

TWO
I want to be the Mommy.

ONE
No, I'm the Mommy, because the Mommy is smart, and she runs everything, but she has to pretend she can't fix the toaster.

THREE
I'll be the Daddy and snore.

TWO
And I'm Super-Girl, and everybody thinks I'm Kathy, but really I was born on another planet, and the planet exploded, and I journey to a distant star.

ONE
Wow. Then what?

TWO
Then I'm disguised as a little brat.

They join hands.

ONE
Ok, here's our time machine, and then we're a family.

They rotate: "One, two, three. . ." Circle explodes. They freeze, look around, confused, then rush into line facing audience. They join hands, raise hands to audience. In unison:

ALL
WE ARE A FAMILY.

They drop hands, speak individually to audience.

FATHER
Husband and father.

MOTHER
Just a housewife.

DAUGHTER
I'm a junior this year.

FATHER *(patting his belly)*
Just a growing boy.

They present clasped hands.

ALL
WE ARE A FAMILY.

They drop hands, speak.

FATHER
I enjoy a good brandy.

DAUGHTER
I smoke a little dope.

MOTHER
I have some pills for depression.

DAUGHTER
But I really just get high on living.

They present clasped hands.

ALL
WE ARE A FAMILY.

They drop hands, speak.

MOTHER
I like classical music.

FATHER
Easy listening.

MOTHER
Peace and quiet.

DAUGHTER
Anything loud.

They present clasped hands.

ALL
WE ARE A FAMILY.

They drop hands, speak.

FATHER
I work hard for a living.

DAUGHTER
I sponge.

MOTHER
I shop the sales.

DAUGHTER
I shop. . .lift.

They present clasped hands.

ALL
WE ARE A FAMILY.

They drop hands, speak.

FATHER
I eat whatever's on the table.

MOTHER
I'm always on a diet.

DAUGHTER
I like really spicy food.

All shift, Father and Mother to sides.

I had a boyfriend that's Italian, and over at his house, there's always about a million kids, and they're all smeared with garlic and onions. But here, everything's so bland. The stuff my mom cooks, it tastes like boiled worms.

MOTHER
The first word my daughter learned was "Yuck." I used to try to cook. "What's that smelly stuff?" "Well, it's a little garlic." "Yuck." Or "What's that? I don't like it." "Why not?" "Because I can taste it. Yuck."

DAUGHTER
But it used to be we'd have supper together, and it felt like a family. But now I grab something, and my dad gobbles, and my mom's eating yogurt in the kitchen, and I mean, at meals it should feel like a Family.

All converge, present clasped hands.

ALL

WE *ARE* A FAMILY.

They drop hands, speak.

MOTHER

We belong to First Methodist.

DAUGHTER

Our minister got a divorce.

FATHER

I believe you're judged by your deeds.

DAUGHTER

I still believe in Santa Claus.

They present clasped hands.

ALL

WE ARE A FAMILY.

They regroup for a family portrait, smiling.

MOTHER

Ready now, smile!

Freeze. Speaking, they break tableau, then return.

DAUGHTER

My family's such a bunch of stereotypes. Wind up the Daddy doll—

FATHER

Just wait until you have kids.

DAUGHTER

Wind up the Mommy—

MOTHER

I was saving that for lunch.

DAUGHTER

Wind up the baby: "I want a family. . ." I want a *real* family. My boyfriend joined the Moonies.

Tableau, smiling.

ALL

FAMILYYYYY!

New positions, all upstaged. Mother turns front.

MOTHER

I don't understand politics, but something's got to change. I think what is happening to the country, what is happening to the family. Something has got to change.

She turns upstage, Daughter forward.

DAUGHTER
My dad's a Republican. Can you believe it? A Republican!

She turns upstage, Father forward.

FATHER
Well I can't really justify it, it just came over me. I went into the voting booth and I pulled the curtain and I started to push the lever . . . and I looked . . . and I took out a pencil and I wrote in . . . "Superman."

All converge, arms around shoulders, jovial.

ALL
WE ARE A FAMILY.

FATHER
I try to set a good example.

DAUGHTER
My dad's been playing around.

MOTHER
With my daughter, it's boys, boys, boys.

DAUGHTER
I think I'm gay.

Silence. Very quiet, halting.

ALL
WE . . . ARE . . . A . . .

Group explodes angrily, two speaking as third continues shouting, mute.

DAUGHTER
It's my room and my records and I can play them if I want!

FATHER
Forty times a day? Why don't you get some new high-quality garbage? Peter Popper and the Pimples—

DAUGHTER
Stop it!

FATHER
Sammy Snotnose and the Sniffs—

DAUGHTER
Stop it!

FATHER
Don't give me your smart mouth, young lady!

DAUGHTER
Leave me alone!

FATHER
You don't talk to your father like that!

DAUGHTER
Ima no talka like dat, Ima talka like dis, cause you my poppa and Ima you little bambina—

FATHER
Ok!

DAUGHTER
An my papacito he wear de grande sombrero, and he maka mucho de pesetas—

FATHER
Stop it!

MOTHER
Do you have to shout! Can't you talk? Can't you communicate?

FATHER
Communicate? I am communicating. I'm standing here communicating. I am communicating as hard as I can!

MOTHER
You call that communication?

DAUGHTER
Well it's my records.

MOTHER
You started this.

DAUGHTER
I'm sorry.

MOTHER
You're sorry all right.

DAUGHTER
Stop making that stupid joke.

MOTHER
Stupid mommy stupid baby.

DAUGHTER
Mother, no—

MOTHER
You're sorry. You're flunking in school. You're lazy. Your hair is a mess. You need a bath. Your room is the city dump.

You're surly, you're ungrateful, you don't have one redeeming feature, you've brought me nothing but grief! Sometimes I wish you'd never been born!

DAUGHTER *(very quietly)*
All right. I'll go. I'll get out of your life. I'm going. I'm gone.

MOTHER *(plaintive)*
But honey . . . you're our daughter.

Slowly they shift, Mother and Daughter upstage, Father down center.

ALL
WE . . . ARE . . . A . . . FAMILY . . .

Silence.

FATHER
When I was a kid, I had the distinct impression that adults could cope.

He shrugs.

Once my uncle gave me a quarter. I was so happy. A quarter! I took it, I went down, I bought the biggest candy bar they had. A Bit-o-Honey. Never had a Bit-o-Honey. Family Size, but not for the family: all mine.

And I'll always remember. I took it, I tore off the wrapper, I bit into it, and it's honey nougat. I hate honey nougat. That's how I feel. I got it all, and I can't swallow it.

Triangle revolves, leaving Daughter down center.

ALL
WE . . . ARE . . . A . . . FAMILY . . .

DAUGHTER
I am so very afraid that I will screw up my life. I mean, what about school? What about sex? What about a career?

And I know . . . I know that I am going to do the Safe Thing. I am going to Be Sensible. I am going to Use My Head. I am going to Be a Nerd.

Jeez, I don't care if I'm an airline pilot or drive a garbage truck or join the Marines or have ten kids. I just want to be alive. I want things to be loud, and funny, and lots of spice and bright colors and—

If I could only talk to my mom. But I can't. She's never lived. She's never felt anything. She's never lived.

MOTHER
Then how does she think she came into the world?

Triangle revolves, leaving Mother down center.

ALL
WE . . . ARE . . . A . . . FAMILY . . .

MOTHER
I did the craziest thing. Everybody was gone, out somewhere. And I just left the dishes. I turned off the set. I did not lock the door. I don't think I believed I was going to do it. I felt like a shameless woman. I didn't know how you go about these things. . .

I went roller skating. Well I hadn't done it for twenty-five years. I pretended I was young. I walked in, and there were all these teenagers. I've never been so embarrassed. But I rented the skates, with my head held high, and I skated. I did not fall down. I skated. I looked so silly, it was wonderful.

Mother, in mime, begins to skate.

FATHER *(distant)*
I need some clean underwear!

MOTHER
All afternoon. . .

DAUGHTER *(distant)*
She doesn't understand!

MOTHER
Isn't it disgraceful?

FATHER *(distant)*
What's for dessert?

MOTHER
This is dessert. This is my dessert. My just dessert.

All skate in slow motion, converging.

DAUGHTER
I'm skating . . . Super Skater . . . from a distant star. . .

MOTHER
I like to go slow. . .

FATHER
One leg . . . one leg. . .

Off balance, they join hands. Freeze in tableau.

ALL

WE ARE A FAMILY.

Gently they unclasp hands, standing, side by side.

DAUGHTER

I love my father.

FATHER

I love my wife.

MOTHER

I love my daughter.

They present clasped hands. Silence. Blackout.

Stoplight

Note: in The Independent Eye's performance, the child is represented by a rag doll, manipulated by an actress, who speaks her lines.

Dad and small Child stand hand in hand at a street corner. Dad leans down, points.

DAD
Ok now, before we cross. Here. Look. Ok, can you read that?

CHILD
"Walk."

DAD
Great. Ok, now wait just a second, till the light changes, and you can try that. You ready? Ok?

CHILD
"Don't Walk."

DAD
That's great. Wow. You're a reader. That's terrific. And ok, now when it says that, then you don't walk. It says Walk and you walk, and Don't Walk, and then you stay here and let the cars go. Ok? That's great.
Ok, let's cross now. Hold onto my hand.

CHILD *(holding back)*
Daddy—

DAD
Huh?

CHILD
It says Don't Walk.

DAD
Right, fine, that's true, but I mean right now we're in a hurry now, and it's ok if you're with Daddy and you hold onto my hand.

Pause.

I mean it's not something you ought to do, but we're ok, there aren't any cars coming, but you shouldn't ordinarily cross, I mean, although people do, even when they're not sposed to, and that's called jaywalking, but I'm not saying to do that, but right now we need to or else we're gonna be late, and we want to tell Mommy how well you're learning to read!

Shift to the Child's inner experience. Sudden burst of talk. Confused responses from Child. In the Eye's performance, the Child doll is tossed head over heels in the air.

DAD

Ok, cross now. No, stay. Ok, go. No. Stop. Hurry. Wait. Go. Don't just stand there. Do what I tell you. Obey the law.

Dad freezes. Everything settles. To us:

CHILD

I read ok. But I don't understand the words.

Fade.

Cat in the Attic

A middle-aged couple, in midst of a quarrel.

WOMAN
Well didn't you hear me?

MAN
I was asleep!

WOMAN
I was yelling my head off. I like to died up there!

MAN
You should of waked me up. I'da got the cat out of the attic.

WOMAN
Well you were asleep!

MAN
That's what I'm saying!

WOMAN
Well I didn't know. The cat's up in the attic and I get the ladder, and heave myself up there, only it's the short ladder, and I can't get back down. I was there for three hours, damn it!

MAN
I was asleep!

WOMAN
I yelled and screamed— Didn't you see the note?

MAN
I didn't know what it meant.

WOMAN
It said, "I'm in the attic. I can't get out." What else would it mean?

MAN
It's on the cat's collar.

WOMAN
I figured you'd see the cat, so I put the note on its collar and threw it down outa the attic.

MAN
Well yeh, I saw it. The damn thing climbed onto my face, woke me up—

WOMAN

I just about died up there!

MAN

Well I was asleep!

Shift. They settle into themselves, then speak directly to us:

How I'm sposed to hear her if I'm asleep. She's telling me, "You look tired, take a nap." And then it's "Whatta you doin' asleep?" You can't win.

WOMAN

So the cat wakes him up, and he reads "I'm in the attic," and he says, "Well now you're out," and throws the cat down and goes back to sleep.

They look at each other.

Nobody will ever believe that one.

Blackout.

Mud

Breakfast table. Mom is folding laundry. Kid comes running in.

KID
Momma?

MOM
Finish your cereal.

KID
I did. Can I go out?

MOM
It's wet.

KID
That's ok.

MOM
Why don't you watch cartoons?

KID
They're dumb.

MOM
You might catch cold.

KID
Please.

MOM
No.

KID
Please.

MOM
Why don't you wait a little bit?

KID
Please.

MOM
Well it's wet. You'll get wet and then you'll catch cold and then you'll be very sorry.

KID
I wanta play in the mud. I can't play in the mud if there's not any mud.

MOM
Well. . .

KID
Please!

MOM
Well all right. For a little while. You can play in the mud. And it's fine to play in the mud as long as you remember what you have to do—

KID
Yeh Momma—

MOM
That you have to be careful and remember that Momma works hard to keep you looking your best and healthy and happy and wants you to go out and have a good time with your friends—

KID
Yeh Momma—

MOM
But you have to remember that Momma would be upset if she found you playing in the mud and you hadn't remembered and forgot—

KID
Yeh Momma—

MOM
—That it's ok to play in the mud as long as you keep clean.

He looks at her, totally baffled. She shifts into herself, speaks to us. In the Eye's performance, the actor playing the Kid becomes the voices of the neighbors, intersecting her speech.

MOM
Don't I have to take care of my kid? I got work to do. Instant clean, sure! Look like trash, people treat you like trash.

NEIGHBORS *(simultaneously)*
She's overprotective. She lets that kid run wild. Tied to her apron strings. Some people just shouldn't have kids.

Shift. Mom sits down, exhausted.

MOM
I'd like to be one of those so-and-so's on the detergent commercials. They've always got the answers.

Blackout.

Chicken House

Farm family eating supper. Note: in the Eye staging, the Child is represented by a doll, held by both parents, who speak his lines in unison. Very minimal movement.

CHILD
Mommy?

WOMAN
Finish your peas.

MAN
Don't chase'em around the plate.

Pause.

CHILD
Mommy?

WOMAN
What?

CHILD
Why is Grandpa in the chicken house?

WOMAN
He's not in the chicken house. Finish your food.

CHILD
Why is he?

WOMAN
It's not a chicken house. It used to be a chicken house when he had the farm, but we fixed it up and it's just like any other house.

CHILD
He thinks it's a chicken house.

MAN
Dad? You talking bout Dad?

WOMAN
Well Grandpa thinks funny things. Old people get like that. That's one of the tragedies of life. It's a one-room house. We scrubbed it out, painted it, we take his meals out to him. It's not a chicken house.

MAN

He wouldn't live in the farm house.

WOMAN

We said you want to live here, you can't mess all over, you gotta follow the rules. It was his choice. He coulda followed the rules.

CHILD

Can he come in to supper?

WOMAN

No. Eat your food. It's not a chicken house. We do a lot better for him than most people do for their parents. I work all day, then cook meals, I don't have time to clean up his mess.

MAN

I used to sit right there, he'd haul off and knock me cross the room.

Shift to flashback, Man and Woman quarreling.

WOMAN

Your own father!

MAN

It's not a chicken house.

WOMAN

What are people gonna think?

MAN

I treat him a lot better than he treated me. It's not a chicken house.

WOMAN

It is if you think it is and you're living there.

Shift back to present.

CHILD

Will you live out there some day?

WOMAN

When?

CHILD

When I'm big?

Silence.

May I be excused?

Fade.

Wrappings

Man and woman sort through cardboard boxes in the attic.

KEN
What's that box?

MARTI
Oh God, do we have to go through all this? That's the Christmas wrappings.

KEN *(laughing)*
There's four boxes of it.

MARTI
Kenny, I got through the funeral, and we've been doing this all day, and my plane leaves in three hours. I don't know if I'm up for this right now.

KEN
You wanta leave it for me?

MARTI
No, I guess not. Eight hours to sort through forty years.

KEN
God, every year— "No, that paper, you keep that." "Open it careful so you don't rip the paper."

MARTI
"Keep those bows! Those bows cost money!"

KEN
And then she comes around next year to wrapping presents— "Here, I bought some new wrappings, package of bows—"

MARTI
"Don't use that rumpled old stuff. This is Christmas."

KEN
So do we toss it? Or keep it?

MARTI
Are you kidding?

KEN
Well what's wrong with wrapping new Chrismases in old Chrismases? That's what people do.

Shift. To themselves, reading tags:

MARTI
To Kenny from Mom and Dad.

KEN
To my beloved Wife.

MARTI
To Marti and Kenny from your old Grandpa.

KEN
To Birdbrain from your Brother.

MARTI
To Kenny from your loving Mom.

Shift.

KEN
Ok, so I'll take the wrappings, we'll split the bows. What's the matter?

MARTI
Nothing.

Pause, then a sudden outburst.

Kenny, I'm very appreciative that you made the arrangements. You loved her, you took care of her the last eight years, and that was heroic. It was.

Just remember I was at home with her while you were out to Cub Scouts, and Boy Scouts, and basketball, and run-ins with the cops, and all the crap you put her through.

I put up with more abuse and tears and venom than you will ever know, so I think the score is even. I do.

KEN
I thought that stuff was past. I guess you faked it through the funeral.

MARTI
Right. I faked it.

KEN
You're saying you didn't love her.

MARTI
Right. I did not love my mother vicious and falling-down drunk. But I always got dinner on the table.

Oh, did you run across a little ceramic— I made her a— No, she would have thrown it out.

KEN
I'm sorry.

MARTI

So am I.

Pause. They continue packing. Suddenly, Marti laughs.

Remember when she stabbed Dad in the leg? You were at Scouts, and she started throwing dishes and he said that cost too much and he hit her, and she had the paring knife and stabbed him in the leg.

They went to the hospital and told'em he was opening a beer can with it and it slipped. And then you and me had a fight over who was gonna clean it all up.

Shift. To themselves, as children:

KEN

How do you get blood out of a carpet?

MARTI

Is Sally's mom and dad like this? Is Jennifer's?

KEN

It's sposed to be your turn.

MARTI

I did the dishes. You do the blood.

Back into the scene. He looks at her, bewildered.

KEN

I don't remember that.

MARTI

Well, I survived. And there were nice Christmases.

KEN

So what about the wrappings?

Fade.

HAMMERING

Man hammering nails. Small girl approaches.

In the Eye performance, the girl is represented by a rag doll, perched on the man's shoulder, manipulated by the actress. As the age transition occurs, the actress embodies the character herself.

GIRL
Daddy?

DAD
Hi hon.

GIRL
When can I learn that?

DAD
I'll tell you what, hon. I'm busy right now, but when I have time I'll teach you how to hammer nails and the whole thing, cause it's important you learn how to do things.

GIRL
When can I?

DAD
Well right now I gotta fix these cabinets—
Ok, tell you what. You can hammer this nail for me, ok? Then I gotta work.
Ok, take the hammer. Ok. Now hold the nail like this. Up like that. Now kinda tap on it. Good. Ok—

She drops the hammer.

GIRL
I dropped it.

DAD
Well that's a start. Now I gotta work.

GIRL
When can I learn it?

DAD
When there's time.

GIRL
When?

DAD
Not now.

Hammer. Shift. Girl is older.

AS OLDER GIRL
When?

DAD
Not now.

Hammer. Shift. Girl is a young woman.

AS YOUNG WOMAN
When?

DAD
Not now.

Hammer. Shift. Girl is a mature woman.

AS WOMAN
When?

DAD
Not now.

Shift. Both actors speak in unison, focused on the doll representing the Girl.

VOICES
She's a little clumsy. She's challenged on eye-hand coordination. She's smart but she gives up on things. She's a klutz.

Shift. The actress is an elderly woman, speaking to the doll as her granddaughter.

AS OLD WOMAN
My father tried to show me how to do stuff. But I never had the aptitude. I can't hammer a nail.

MAN *(to us)*
This was a snapshot brought to you by the next generation, who says. . .

GIRL
Can I try?

Fade.

Sam's Pizza

Distant, a young woman sits, facing away. Opposite, phone rings. Man hurries to answer.

SAM
Sam's Pizza.

GIRL *(on phone)*
Is this the Crisis Line?

SAM
This is Sam's Pizza.

GIRL
I was calling the Crisis Line.

SAM
We're bout to lock up.

GIRL
I need to talk.

SAM
You want a pizza?

GIRL
I'm sorry, I thought I was calling the Crisis Line. You know the number for the Crisis Line?

SAM
No.

GIRL
Oh my God—

SAM
So whatta you got? A crisis?

GIRL
I don't know. I can't think. I had a big fight with my dad—

SAM
Hey, is this a joke?

GIRL
Please talk to me!

SAM
Hey, you ain't gonna commit suicide or something, are you? Cause I don't know how to tell people not to jump off the bridge or something. I didn't go to college.

GIRL

My dad drinks a lot and—

SAM

Look, everybody's got problems. The best thing is, you work it out. My kids are good kids, they grow up, they help me, now they're married, they're doing fine. It all works out.

GIRL

I don't think it will.

SAM

Look, this is Sam's Pizza. I'd talk to you, but they got people for that. I'm not qualified to talk to people. I could get sued.

GIRL

And sometimes he comes in and— I try not to— And last night he said if I wouldn't, he'd go to my little sister. . .

SAM *(after a moment)*

Talk to your mother. Talk to your aunts and uncles. That's what a family's for. Don't talk to me.

GIRL

Please!

SAM *(calling off)*

Hold on, I'm on the phone!

GIRL

Please.

SAM *(calling off)*

No, it's two extra large, pepperoni. No, no anchovies.

GIRL

Please talk to me. Please. My birthday's on Saturday.

SAM

Pepperoni. No damn anchovies! *(to phone)* Hey, ok, look, I'm sorry, so talk, I'll try to—

Her phone dangles by its cord. Dial tone.

WOMAN *(off)*

Who is it?

SAM

Wrong number.

Hangs up. To us:

Well I tried.

Fade.

Thanks

Three at dinner table. Mom enraged, Girl in tears, Dad trying to ignore the quarrel.

MOM
I mean it!

DAD
Could we just eat?

MOM
So eat!

DAD
I'm trying.

GIRL
Mom, I'll do it.

MOM
You already said that.

GIRL
So whatta you want me to say?

MOM
I want you to do it! Stop saying it and do it!

DAD
Pass the potatoes?

MOM
Louise is your aunt, and she's my sister, and she sent you a birthday present, and she deserves a thank-you note—

GIRL
I don't know what to say!

MOM
Say thank you!

DAD *(taking dish)*
Thanks.

GIRL
I can't just say that. It's stupid.

MOM
"Thank you for the lovely present. I like it. I'm so overwhelmed I'm speechless. Yours truly." Just write it! She called and asked "Did Sally get the present?" I was so embarrassed!

GIRL

Why? It's my business! I could write it if you didn't keep nagging!

MOM

If you just followed through with one thing you ever say you're gonna do— You say you'll do it, and then you don't, and then I nag, and then you feel persecuted—

I'll write it for you!

GIRL

No!

DAD

Is there any dessert?

Shift. Girl, by herself, tries to write.

GIRL

"Well hey, thanks for the—" I never asked her for it.

"Mom says write you this note—" All it does is make me feel guilty.

"It's the most beautiful—" Oh God—

DAD

Hey. Just fake it.

GIRL

"Thank you. For the thing."

Blackout.

MEDICAL HISTORY

Doctor at desk. Young Woman sitting opposite.

DOCTOR
Ok, so let's see— You haven't been here before—

WOMAN
I haven't had a general physical for, wow, long time. When I was pregnant, they said there was some enlargement of the kidneys, maybe cysts or something, I should check it periodically—

DOCTOR
Any history of kidney problems in your family?

WOMAN
I don't really know anything about medical history. I'm adopted.

DOCTOR
You didn't fill anything out here. They never told you?

WOMAN
My adoptive parents got no information.

DOCTOR
Well you should get the records. Family history can be very important with a lot of things, kidneys for one.

WOMAN
I know.

DOCTOR
So—

WOMAN
The records are sealed at adoption. Court order. I have inquired. I would like that information, for precisely that reason—

DOCTOR
You have children?

WOMAN
Two.

DOCTOR
Well you really should get those records—

WOMAN
I've tried—

DOCTOR
If not for your own sake, for the sake of the children.

WOMAN

It's against the law. I have no rights. The records are sealed. It's a brick wall.

DOCTOR

Well that's your decision, but I'm just telling you from a medical standpoint—

WOMAN

The law says I have no right to the knowledge of my medical history!

DOCTOR

Well it's up to you.

Pause.

So let's check your blood pressure.

Shift to another reality. Rapid fire, intersecting with Woman's ad lib responses.

Any history of breast cancer? Diabetes? History of high blood pressure? Kidney disease? Cardiac problems? Epilepsy? Depression? Cystic fibrosis? Ovarian cancer?

WOMAN

I don't know.

Shift back.

DOCTOR

Well then we'd better do some tests.

WOMAN

Send me the bill.

Blackout.

Hot Fudge

Brother and Sister — full-grown adults — enter from opposite sides of stage. They rush about, searching, then converge center stage, facing upstage, shouting upstairs.

BROTHER

Mom! Will you get out of the bathroom, Mom?

SISTER

Mom, me too! Get out of the bathroom, Mom!

BROTHER

Mom, I said it first, Mom. Get out of the bathroom! *(to Sister)* You don't have to pee just because I have to pee.

SISTER

I don't have to pee. Mom, get out of the bathroom and fix supper! I'm hungry!

BROTHER

I need the car keys, Mom. Get out of the bathroom and give me the car keys!

SISTER

I'm hungry, Mom!

BROTHER

I need the car keys and some money, Mom!

SISTER

Steak well done and cut all the fat off, and a hot fudge sundae!

BROTHER *(to Sister)*

What do you think she is, a waitress?

BOTH

MOM!

They face off.

BROTHER

Every time you take a breath you're asking Mom for something, and you get it too. She's always cooking you things and getting you things—

SISTER

You got a transistor radio and a motorbike and a camera and a stereo—

BROTHER
I didn't want a stereo, I wanted a color TV! I never get what I want. She never bought me anything I really wanted, cause she's always in the kitchen cooking food for you.

SISTER
She cooks me yucky food! I don't like the slop she feeds me. It's yucky, Mom! She makes me eat peas. Peas, carrots, potatoes, rutabagas. I just want dessert. Get out of the bathroom, Mom, I want a hot fudge sundae!

BOTH
MOM!

BROTHER
She always liked you the best.

SISTER
She hates me and she likes you because you're a big fake.

BROTHER
I'm nice to her and you're not— *(screaming)* Mom!

SISTER
Get out of the bathroom, Mom!

BROTHER
Give me keys and give me money!

SISTER
Fix me some yucky supper!

BROTHER *(to Sister)*
Will you stop your screaming!

BOTH
MOM!

Suddenly they look up the stairs. In mime, they watch Mom fall downstairs at their feet, dead.

BROTHER
Look what you did now.

SISTER
Coronary thrombosis.

BROTHER
You had it coming.

SISTER
You reaped what you sowed.

Both fold hands, step over the imaginary corpse, stand as if at a funeral.

BROTHER
They're looking this way.

SISTER
Act sad.

BROTHER
She never loved me. She died before I finished college.

SISTER
Mom's dead. I'm really broken up.

BROTHER
Me too.

SISTER
You don't have to be broken up just because I'm broken up.

BROTHER
I didn't know you cared.

SISTER
Well I do. And you know what would really ease my mind. *(whispering)* A hot fudge sundae.

BROTHER
At a funeral?

SISTER
Well, when I get like this, all broken up and shit, I get hungry.

BROTHER
Serves you right.

SISTER
Yeh? Well, I got something you don't.

BROTHER
What?

She shows.

The car keys! Give me the car keys! Mom, make her give me the— Beg your pardon. *(in an undertone)* I'll give you my stereo if you give me the car keys.

SISTER
I only want one thing.

BROTHER
Anything.

SISTER
Drive me down to the Dairy Queen. Now!

BROTHER
Right!

SISTER
Mom! I'm gonna get ten hot fudge sundaes! And I'm not going to eat any peas! Ha!

BROTHER
I'm gonna burn rubber, Mom! I'm gonna drive her wide open!

BOTH
STAY IN THERE, MOM!

They mime getting in the car, speed away madly.

SISTER
Come on, hurry. I can taste it now.

BROTHER
This baby is mo-o-ving! Watch me go round that cop!

SISTER
There's the Dairy Queen.

BROTHER
Now I'm gonna really open it up.

SISTER
Hey, you gotta turn.

BROTHER
No hands!

SISTER *(struggling with steering wheel)*
Turn in there!

BROTHER
We're coming into the Dairy Queen—

SISTER
Right into the . . . HOT FUDGE! YAAAAH!

They crash, sprawl, dead. Slowly, they raise their heads. Look around, respond to the scenery.

BROTHER
Is something burning?

SISTER
Oh. Hell.

BROTHER
I guess I missed the turn.

SISTER
"I guess I missed the turn."

BROTHER
Well, you wanted a hot topping. You got it. You got your just dessert.

SISTER
Are they gonna make me eat peas?

BROTHER
Can I get the car fixed? Must be a lotta mechanics down here.

SISTER
Where's Mom? She'll take care of it.

BROTHER
Mom!

BOTH
MOM!!!

Silence.

BROTHER
What are you laughing about?

SISTER
I'm not laughing. Who's laughing? Who the hell is laughing?

They look around. Finally look up.

BROTHER
It's Mom.

SISTER
Mom. Mom! Your stupid son wrecked the car!

BROTHER
Mom, that makeup job on you looks terrible!

SISTER
She's smiling. What are you smiling about?

BROTHER
She's got. . . She's got wings! Chrome wings! A four barrel carb and a racing cam! Mom!

SISTER
Wait. . . There's a cloud going by. . . There she is. . . She's. . . She's eating a . . . hot fudge sundae! She's up there and she's got a hot fudge sundae! Mom, drip some down!

BOTH
MOM!

Howl. Long pause. Their heads droop onto one another's shoulders. Grieving unison:

This is hell.

Blackout.

TRIVIA

Man and Woman sit side by side on sofa. They're playing Trivial Pursuit, but there are no cards, no game: it's ingrained.

MAN
What country borders Bolivia to the north?

WOMAN
Iraq. Who was the announcer on the Sid Caesar Show?

MAN
Walter Cronkite. What was Abraham Lincoln's middle name?

WOMAN
Delano. Who was the first golfer to earn a million?

MAN
Joe Louis. What happened to Little Miss Muffitt?

WOMAN
Put her in a pumpkin shell. Where is Candlestick Park?

MAN
The Poconos. What—

Pause.

WOMAN
What?

MAN
Why are we doing this?

WOMAN
Can you think of something better?

MAN
Are these things stuff we really want to know?

WOMAN
You want to talk about something?

MAN
Can't we do better than this?

WOMAN
Is it my turn?

MAN
Isn't there more to life than this?

WOMAN
You want me to answer that?

Pause.

MAN
Well actually I guess not. What was Count Basie's real name?

WOMAN
Ludwig. What is the scientific name of Lou Gehrig's Disease?

MAN
Mumps. Who was the fifth Beatle?

WOMAN
Zeppo. Is this ever going to stop?

MAN
I don't remember.

Shift into inner reality. They speak to us.

WOMAN
I just find it hard to express what I really want to say.

MAN
I'm not sure how she might react.

WOMAN
It might open up a real can of worms.

MAN
I might sound dumb.

WOMAN
I don't pretend to have all the answers.

Shift back. They look at each other.

BOTH
Gotcha!

Blackout.

COFFEE SHOP

Man in his early thirties, Woman about the same age, drinking coffee.

MAN
You met him, didn't you? Dave?

WOMAN
Just briefly, I think, was it Baltimore?

MAN
Yeh, at that time we were just seeing each other, then about two years ago, Groundhog's Day, in fact— Was that after you moved?

WOMAN
Yeh.

MAN
Yeh. And we really made a commitment. And great. And like three months later—

WOMAN
Did he already know he had it then?

MAN
I think so. He wasn't always totally honest. In fact he was kinda hard to take. And then he'd surprise you.

Pause.

You remember when I called, and you said come over to supper, so I did, and then Jodie went off to bed—

WOMAN
And you were just getting up to go, I got the call about my dad.

MAN
He had a stroke or something—

WOMAN
And I said, "Just hold me." And you did. Of course I remember.

MAN
And you know Dave was really jealous, I mean like paranoid sometimes, and so I came home late, and he said, "Where were you?" And so I told him.

And I told him we'd hugged, and you talked about your dad, and it was totally innocent, and same time it was, God, one of the

most intimate times I've ever had with any human being.
It was suddenly being family.

WOMAN
It was.

MAN
And he just said, "I love you."

Pause.

And I took care of him, and the last five months were very difficult. He didn't have insurance and of course mine didn't cover, but I paid quite a lot.
And then he went to intensive care, and— They wouldn't let me be with him. "Only his immediate family."
I washed him and cleaned him and nursed him for months and—

WOMAN
What about his mom and dad? Wouldn't they help?

MAN
He would not allow me to ask them. He didn't want to be a burden to his family.

WOMAN
His family.

MAN
God, Sally. . . What does it take to be family?

Shift. Voices in their heads. In the Eye performance, the two actors, faced away and down, speak these lines in unison, in styles ranging from political speech to Gregorian chant to cartoon.

VOICES
The question is, to give all relationships the status of the family unit, will that undermine the strength of the family unit?
Where does the family derive its strength?
What the hell is the family unit?
What does it take to be family?

Shift. To each other:

MAN
More coffee?

WOMAN
Want to split a piece of that cheesecake?

Fade.

The Grades

Dad and Son in the car, Son driving. They are in midst of an argument.

DAD

I don't believe it. What about your grades?

SON

My grades are fine.

DAD

Your grades are terrific. Your test scores— You got the highest test scores they ever had.

SON

Is that my fault?

DAD

So you throw it all away.

SON

Am I dropping you at the hardware store?

DAD

Post office. You were accepted at Brown, Penn State—

SON

I didn't want to apply—

DAD

You were accepted!

Pause. Driving.

SON

Dad, I said it for a year. I don't want to. You always said the thing is be happy.

DAD

If you worked my damn job— College is the way up!

SON

To what? I don't want to spend four years writing papers about *Moby Dick*—

DAD

That guy's turning, slow down—

SON

I go to community college two years, work part-time, come out doing what I want to do.

DAD
Fixing cars.

SON
Fixing cars.

DAD
You're too smart for that.

SON
So, are only dummies supposed to do useful stuff? You want a dummy to fix your new car?

DAD
One just did.

SON
Dad, I know what's right for me. I don't think it's low class to get your hands greasy. I don't think you're low-class.

DAD
Your problem is you're too damn smart.

Son sighs. Shift to inner reality. They speak to us:

DAD
What did I do wrong?

SON
Why does he think he did something wrong?

DAD
There's a difference between low class and upper class.

SON
Why can't he trust me?

DAD
Maybe he'll grow out of it. Maybe one of us will.

Shift back.

SON
Here's your stop.

DAD
Just pull over.

SON
Well I mean like, thanks, or whatever. . .

They look at each other. Fade.

Joellen & Willie

Kitchen. Mother and Daughter quarreling.

WILLIE
Mom!—

JOELLEN
I'm just telling you—

WILLIE
I heard you, you're telling me over and over—

JOELLEN
I want you to listen!

WILLIE
Mom!

JOELLEN
What about my question?

WILLIE
I went out for a ride.

JOELLEN
You just go for rides where you don't have any idea what they do, beer and marijuana—

WILLIE
The grass was Chuck's.

JOELLEN
Oh I'm glad to know that. That's a whole lot better. The grass was Chuck's.

You're not making this easy. Willie, you're fifteen. You go out with an older man—

WILLIE
He's not older—

JOELLEN
Six years—

WILLIE
Seven.

JOELLEN
Run a red light, cops call me down there— God, I sound like my mother.

Pause. They recover.

Honey, I'm not trying to run your life. I just want a good life for you. A better life than I had, and it's so easy to mess up—
I know you're smart. You're smarter than I was at your age, and when you start to get serious about some young man—
You have the advantage, cause you can learn from my mistakes.

WILLIE
What mistakes?

JOELLEN
Just things I did that. . . I would have been better off not doing.

WILLIE
Like what?

JOELLEN
Just things that I did at your age that at the time I didn't know any better and I thought I was so smart—

WILLIE
What?

JOELLEN
Huh?

WILLIE
You said learn from your mistakes. So what mistakes?

JOELLEN
Mistakes! None of your business! Never mind! Shut up!

Willie sighs. Shift to inner dialogue, to us:

WILLIE
All she does is nag. She never listens. She never says anything.

JOELLEN
I'm scared to death.

WILLIE
She's a total hypocrite.

JOELLEN
My kid's too much like me.

Shift back. Willie rises.

WILLIE
I'm going out.

JOELLEN
No you're not.

WILLIE
I am.

JOELLEN
I say no.

WILLIE
I'm going.

JOELLEN *(giving up)*
Ok. You've got your key.

WILLIE
You can't stop me.

JOELLEN
Nope. You've got your key. Ok. Go.

Suspended silence.

WILLIE
You don't really care, do you?

JOELLEN *(at a loss)*
I must have been fifteen once, but by God I can't remember.

WILLIE *(enraged, in tears)*
I feel so . . . ridiculous!

She sits down. Again, shift to inner:

If she'd just shut up. If she'd just talk to me. If she'd just mind her own business. If she'd just treat me like a grownup.

JOELLEN
If we just get through this year.

Shift back. Joellen rises, going off to bed.

JOELLEN
There's some fresh strawberries, Willie. 'Night.

WILLIE
Thank you.

Joellen out. Fade.

THE ANSWER

Mother and teenage daughter, in the kitchen, doing dishes.

SHEILA
Hand me those plates. So what you wanta know?

KIM
Like, the whole thing.

SHEILA
That's gonna sound pretty funny for a school report. Scrape that off a little better.

KIM
I want to do something that matters.

SHEILA
Well just make it clear I was married. That's old-fashioned, maybe, but I was married. Three years.

KIM
Ok.

SHEILA
Well I told you before.

KIM
Well I want to get it right.

SHEILA
Well what I said. I was pregnant. I came down with German measles, they said "Your baby might be deformed." We were in Galveston, I could have gone out of state to do it, but I was working, I didn't. I decided to keep the baby.

So then at delivery, there was this real long pause while the doctor examined the baby. Examined you. Finally said "Your daughter is perfect."

The one thing I wasn't prepared for was that. I started shaking. I thought I was going to fall apart.

Drops dish. It breaks.

Damn. Broken dish and a runny nose. Thanks a lot.

Shift to inner reality, speaking to themselves.

KIM
I might not be here.

SHEILA
She might not of had a face.

KIM
I might not had arms.

SHEILA
She mighta lived brain-dead for twenty years.

KIM
I might still be happy.

SHEILA
She's perfect.

KIM
I might wanta die.

Shift back. Sheila picks up the pieces. Kim stacks plates.

Well anyway, thanks for telling me.

SHEILA
So what would you have done? If you was me?

KIM
Can I do a report where I don't know the answer?

Fade.

GOING OUT

Man and Woman, sitting on the sofa, staring straight ahead.

WOMAN
Could we get out of the house tonight. I'm going stir crazy.

MAN
Sure, no problem. Good casserole.

WOMAN
There's something about the suburbs. Like a life sentence.

MAN
With a thirty-year mortgage. Ok, where to? Movie?

WOMAN
Probably not anything I want to see. Bunch of gum-popping kids.

MAN
Theatre?

WOMAN
That's such a hassle. Dress up and then go see something you never heard of, then it's dark you walk back to your car.

MAN
Hey! Ball game!

WOMAN
Can't tell who you're going to be sitting next to. How about someplace and listen to music?

MAN
Clear downtown. They put these places where it's not safe to go. Get your car broke into.

WOMAN
Something going on at the college?

MAN
Well you have to drive there too. Read about these car-jackings.

WOMAN
Well I'd just like to see some people.

MAN
We're having the Johnsons over on Friday.

WOMAN
I mean real people.

MAN
That's what talk shows are for.

WOMAN
What if we go out and do some drive-by shootings?

MAN
That's an idea.

Shift to inner dialogue.

WOMAN
There's too much traffic.

MAN
Too many people.

WOMAN
Too many kinds of people.

MAN
Everything's too crowded.

WOMAN
Kinds of people you never know.

MAN
We never see anybody any more.

They turn to each other.

How bout I rent a video?

WOMAN
Is the back door locked?

Blackout.

Love

Three actors, two women and a man. Chairs spaced, facing front. Rapid rhythm.

ONE

Love.

TWO

Love conquers all.

THREE

Love makes the world go round.

TWO

Love is the coldest of critics.

ONE

Love is the orbit of the restless soul.

THREE

Love is a flame.

ONE

Love is a greater law.

TWO

Love is blind.

ONE

Love is not love which alters when it alteration finds, or bends with the remover to remove.

TWO

Love stings.

THREE

Love is a greased pig.

ONE

Alas my love you do me wrong—

TWO

Frankie and Johnny were lovers—

THREE

Everybody loves a lover—

ONE

All we need is love.

THREE

Love.

TWO

Love.

Shift. New characters. Each interrupts the last.

THREE

Cause I love it when Mama says goodnight, she really loves me, they all do. Papa, Mama, Grandma, Teddy Bear, Cookie Monster loves me, the mailman, they all really—

ONE

Stink! Cause they get mad if I don't blow my nose or get all A's, or if I sock the babysitter, and my brother says, "You better stop crying cause nobody loves a crybaby," and I feel so—

TWO

Wiggly inside. I mean is that how it feels? I mean can you really fall in love before you wear a bra? I sit at my desk and try to concentrate but it's just not easy to remember the capital of Idaho when you feel—

ONE

Like a real stud. I mean sure it's my dad's car, but I tell'em it's mine, and I start hitting up around seventy-five, eighty, they're so scared they gotta hang onto my neck, and when I'm up to ninety, they're ready!

Freeze. Shift. Two speak in soft unison.

THREE

What do you think about when you hear the word LOVE?

ALL

Family. Heart. Feeling. Rain. Patience. Pain. Marriage. Flowers. Summer. Birth. Death. Magic.

ONE *(simultaneously)*

I think when I was seven, and I crawled up inside a pillowcase, all wadded up, and my family was at the table, and I waddled out like a little duck-walking marshmallow, and they all cracked up. I felt like I'd done something so neat, they all loved me so much, all I could do was curl up and get hugged.

ALL

Anger. Cats. Mama. Sex. Hair. Rainbows. Tears. Eyes.

THREE *(simultaneously)*

I think why can't you go up to someone and say what you need and it's a law they have to say ok and they don't tell anybody or charge anything and they always have to say I love you.

ALL

Losing. Forever. Alarm clocks. Giggles. Sniffles. Whispers. Mumbles. Rustles. Squeaks. Smells. Tickles. Spring.

TWO *(simultaneously)*

Making love. I think, how do you "make" love? I thought it was something you fell into, like you don't watch on the sidewalk and you step in something.

But then you have all this love, a lifetime supply, and you run through it like a case of beer. Drink it up, and all you can do then is make it. Learn how to make it. One stitch at a time.

Silence. Shift. Two sit as a young couple.

THREE

But that's all we need. Sure there's problems, money and if the job's gonna last. But the car's ok, and he's not drinking, and I can work another couple months. It's gonna be a lot different when the baby comes, just a lot more reason to stick with it—

ONE

Sure there's problems. Money, the car, the baby, I mean it's hard to have the same kind of relationship once there's kids, and she bitches if I have a drink. But we really love each other, and I think if we're really committed to each other then we can work out whatever—

THREE

Kind of settlement we can agree on. Because we finally realized, ok, it's over. It's all fun and games before the kids come, but as soon as he has to start acting like a grownup, then he weasels around and you realize: Hey, I'm alone.

Silence. Shift. Many characters.

ALL

I fell in love—

ONE

But we were still in college.

ALL

I fell in love—

THREE

But the children came first.

ALL

I fell in love—

TWO
Till the first time he hit me.

ALL
I fell in love—

ONE
But once was enough.

ALL
I fell in love—

THREE
But he didn't have Social Security.

ALL
I fell in love—

ONE
Supporting three kids.

ALL
I fell in love—

THREE
But it was a woman.

ALL
I fell in love—

TWO
But not enough.

ALL
I fell in love—

ONE
Again.

Freeze. Shift. All are middle-aged.

TWO
I'm alone. And I don't really mind being alone, remember all the hassles. Oh sometimes you wish somebody would give a damn. But I really find a lot more satisfaction in—

ONE
This relationship than the last one. It's a more mature kind of love. We both do the dishes, we belong to ourselves. It's really a partnership, more of a—

THREE
Business relationship. We have developed this deep financial intimacy that binds us together. The house, insurance, straight life, cash value life, and you don't expect as much—

ONE

You expect a little more! You want somebody to give you—

THREE

The most beautiful valentine. Not just Be My Valentine, but one with a quilted heart and this really reeky perfume, and it costs five dollars and comes right out and says I Love You, and you're not embarrassed at all, you're just—

TWO

Too embarrassed. To reach out and touch and say we're here, for better or worse—

ONE

Better or worse—

THREE

Better. Worse.

Shift. Two sit as an elderly couple.

ONE

I see the Spragues celebrated their golden.

TWO

I should send them a card. They sent us one.

ONE

How's your kidneys now?

TWO

Stop that.

ONE

What?

TWO

That noise you're making.

ONE

Never could tell what they saw in each other.

TWO

Nobody else would have 'em.

ONE

They hate each other and stay together to prove it.

TWO

They sent us a card: "Now your love is flecked with silver."

ONE

Flecked?

TWO
I should send them a card.

ONE
Send 'em the same one back. Flecked.

TWO
Hey. Did you get me a valentine?

ONE
Oh, you think I want to Be Your Valentine?

TWO
Oh, I got some idea. Night before last.

They look at each other, smile.

ONE
Hey. Did you hear Jessie's kids? "You're not my valentine. You're a booger."

TWO
"I'm not a booger."

ONE
"Boogerboogerbooger."

TWO
Well. Even a booger can be a valentine.

Laugh. Shift. Many characters.

ALL
If he loved me—

THREE
He'd make a pot of coffee.

ALL
If she loved me—

ONE
She'd make the toilet bowl sparkle.

ALL
If he loved me—

TWO
He wouldn't wear long johns.

ALL
If she loved me—

THREE
She'd grin and bear it.

ALL
If he loved me—

ONE
He'd see how rotten I am.

ALL
If she loved me—

TWO
I wouldn't have gas.

ALL
If they loved me—

THREE
It wouldn't snow.

ALL
If he loved me—

ONE
He'd grow up.

ALL
If she loved me—

TWO
She'd understand.

ALL
If they loved me—

THREE
I'd love them.

ALL
If they loved me—

ONE
I couldn't believe it.

ALL
If they loved me—

TWO
I'd have to begin.

ALL
If they loved me—

THREE
I'd stand there, tickled pink, and I'd say. . . "Hello."

Fade.

Conrad Bishop & Elizabeth Fuller, after five years of college teaching, were co-founders of Milwaukee's Theatre X and in 1974 formed The Independent Eye, which they continue to direct. They have collaborated in writing more than 60 produced plays. *Wanna* was showcased at the 1980 O'Neill National Playwrights Conference; and *Dreambelly*, produced by Theatre X, toured The Netherlands under auspices of Amsterdam's Mickery Theatre. In 1982, *Full Hookup* was co-winner of Actors Theatre of Louisville's Great American Play Contest, directed by Jon Jory, and had its Off-Broadway premiere at New York's Circle Repertory under the direction of Marshall Mason. *Smitty's News*, directed by Bishop, was presented at the 1986 Humana Festival. Their plays have also been presented by Denver Center Theatre, Mark Taper Forum, Theater of the First Amendment, Asolo Center, Repertory Theatre of St. Louis, Fulton Opera House, Walnut Street Theatre, Cleveland Public Theatre, and many others. They have received five fellowships from Pennsylvania Council on the Arts and were twice recipients of National Endowment for the Arts Playwriting Fellowships.

Their public radio productions include three dramatic series — *The Want Ads*, *Tapdancer*, and *Family Snapshots* — and a documentary series, *Weavers*, and have received many production awards, including the Ohio State Award, a top international broadcast honor.

The Independent Eye is a national touring ensemble, based now in Sebastopol, CA. Since 1974, the Eye has performed in 34 states, has appeared at New York's CSC Rep and Theater for the New City, Chicago's Body Politic, Seattle's New City Theatre, Baltimore Theatre Project, Philadelphia's Painted Bride, and many others, and as focus for social issues forums from Flagstaff to Jerusalem. In 1977, the Eye moved its home from Chicago to Lancaster, PA, opening the Eye Theatre Works in 1982, and from 1992 to 1999 was resident in Philadelphia. Besides touring, the Eye conducts residencies with colleges and high schools, and has developed collaborative productions with many theatres, including Jean Cocteau Repertory, Touchstone Theatre, Theater of the First Amendment, and Bloomsburg Theatre Ensemble.